"Climate change is one of the more contentious issues addressed by policy makers, scientists and pundits today. With so much information on both sides of the debate, it is hard for the average citizen to know what to do. In this short, very readable book, the authors have cut through much of the debate and presented from the Christian perspective what we know about climate change, where the issues still remain and what—when faced with remaining uncertainty—we as Christians should do to respond prayerfully and faithfully to issues of creation care. The thoughtful and prayerful approach taken by our Christian brothers and sisters at Wheaton stands as an example for us all to emulate."

—BEN L. CAMPBELL, Program Director,
Faith-based Initiative, Conservation International

"Wheaton has preformed a great service to evangelicals by spotlighting our responsibility to steward God's wonderful creation. This collection of papers identifies—with neither sugarcoating nor hysteria—the staggering consequences of poor environmental stewardship. The blend of scientific, social, economic, theological, and human perspectives is honest, riveting, and challenging. This collection will convict you of our believers' responsibility for Creation Care; it will challenge you with ways to alter your consumption behaviors."

—PAUL CORTS, President of the Council
for Christian Colleges and Universities

Christians,

the Care of Creation

& Global Climate Change

CHRISTIANS, THE CARE OF CREATION & GLOBAL CLIMATE CHANGE

Edited by
Lindy Scott

☙PICKWICK *Publications* • Eugene, Oregon

CHRISTIANS, THE CARE OF CREATION, AND GLOBAL CLIMATE CHANGE

Copyright © 2008 Wipf and Stock Publishers. All rights reserved. Except for brief quotations in critical publications or reviews, no part of this book may be reproduced in any manner without prior written permission from the publisher. Write: Permissions, Wipf and Stock Publishers, 199 W. 8th Ave., Suite 3, Eugene, OR 97401.

Pickwick Publications
A Division of Wipf and Stock Publishers
199 W. 8th Ave., Suite 3
Eugene, OR 97401

www.wipfandstock.com

ISBN 13: 978-1-55635-844-9

Cataloging-in-Publication data:

Christians, the care of creation, and global climate change / edited by Lindy Scott.

xii + 144 p.; 23 cm.

ISBN 13: 978-1-55635-844-9
Includes bibliographical references.

1. Human ecology—Religious aspects—Christianity. 2. Christian ethics. 3. Global warming—Moral and ethical aspects. 4. Climatic changes—Moral and ethical aspects. I. Scott, Lindy. II. Title.

BT695.5 .C475 2008

Manufactured in the U.S.A.

CONTENTS

Abbreviations vii

Introduction ix
Lindy Scott

PART 1 A Panel Discussion on Global Climate Change

1. Introduction to the Panel Discussion 3
   A. Duane Litfin

2. Is the Sky Falling? 6
   Douglas Allen

3. Global Climate: Implications for Global Health 24
   L. Kristen Page

4. The Economics of Global Warming 36
   P. J. Hill

5. Climate Change: Global Problem, Global Solutions 47
   Noah J. Toly

PART 2 A Christian College Takes Some Initial Steps

6. Big Science, Big God 67
   Sir John T. Houghton

7. The Greening of Wheaton College:
   An Unlikely Tree Hugger 77
   Ben Lowe

8   The Greening of Wheaton College:
    A Bigger Vision   85
    Ben Lowe

9   The Greening of Wheaton College:
    Environment, Economics, and Equity   95
    Vincent E. Morris

    Epilogue: So What? Now What?   124
    Jeffrey K. Greenberg

    List of Contributors   135

    Index   139

ABBREVIATIONS

AOSIS	Alliance of Small Island States
APPCDC	Asia Pacific Partnership on Clean Development and Climate
ASV	American Standard Version (Bible)
AWG	Ad hoc Working Group (of the Kyoto Protocol)
BAU	business-as-usual (adjective)
CACE	Center for Applied Christian Ethics at Wheaton College
CBD	Convention on Biological Diversity
CCP	Cities for Climate Protection
CDM	clean development mechanism
CEC	Christian Environmental Council
CFCs	chlorofluorocarbons
CO_2	carbon dioxide
CO_2e	carbon dioxide equivalent
COP-3	Third Conference on Parties to the UNFCCC
COP-6	Sixth Conference of the Parties to the UNFCCC
CPA	Climate Protection Agreement (of the USCOM)
ECI	Evangelical Climate Initiative
ESA	Endangered Species Act
ESAC	Environmental Stewardship Advisory Committee (at Wheaton College)
ESV	English Standard Version (Bible)
FAR	Fourth Assessment Report of the IPCC
GHG(s)	greenhouse gas(es)
HCFC(s)	hydrofluorocarbon(s)
HPS	hantavirus pulmonary syndrome
ICEL	International Council for Environmental Initiatives
ID	Intelligent Design

IPCC	Intergovernmental Panel on Climate Change
ISCI	International Solar Cities Initiative
ITQ	Individual Transfer Quota
IUCN	World Conservation Union
JI	joint implementation
KJV	King James Version (Bible)
LEED	Leadership in Energy and Environmental Design
NASB	New American Standard Bible (Bible)
NIV	New International Version (Bible)
NOAA	National Oceanic and Atmospheric Administration
NRSV	New Revised Standard Version (Bible)
PERC	Property and Environment Research Center
RGGI	Regional Greenhouse Gas Initiative
SRC	Sports and Recreation Complex
TAR	Third Assessment Report of the IPCC
UNCED	United Nations Conference on Environment and Development
UNFCCC	United Nations Framework Convention on Climate Change
UNFPA	United Nations Population Fund
USCOM	United States Conference of Mayors
UV	Ultraviolet
W/m^2	Watts per square meter
WHO	World Health Organization

INTRODUCTION

Lindy Scott

Imagine that you are sleeping in your cozy bed on a Saturday morning. Your alarm clock awakens you from an enjoyable snooze—but then you realize that it's Saturday and you can sleep in. You reach over to turn off the alarm but accidentally hit the snooze button instead.

Seven minutes later, the alarm goes off again. You wake up, angry to have your beauty sleep interrupted again. But then you remember that you have scheduled the most important meeting of your life for that Saturday morning. Your anger turns to gratitude as you realize that the snooze button woke you up just in time.

This book you have in your hands is just like that snooze-button alarm. It is a wake-up call for Christians and others. It is a cogent and persuasive call to love our God and our neighbors by caring for our Lord's creation—especially in light of the dramatic climate changes occurring before our eyes. This book is not the final word on the subject, but it is a sincere invitation to examine the scientific evidence for global warming and to respond with individual and collective faithful actions.

The first part emerges from a panel discussion held on the campus of Wheaton College on November 13, 2006. Earlier that year, Wheaton's president, Dr. Duane Litfin, had taken an important step by becoming one of the original signatories to the Evangelical Climate Initiative (ECI) statement, "Climate Change: An Evangelical Call to Action." Litfin's action was bold because it affirmed that faithful Christians should respond to the dramatic changes in our climate as part of our holistic discipleship and obedience to God. Following in his steps, the Faculty Advisory Committee of Wheaton's Center for Applied Christian Ethics (CACE) proposed "Environment, Economics and Equity" as the year theme. The panel was one of a series of events sponsored by the ethics center to explore and encourage what faithful discipleship in caring for God's creation. As Litfin introduced the panel and its importance, he articulated his reasons for signing the document and why Wheaton College must not be apathetic on this issue.

Douglas Allen, professor of physics and environmental studies at Dordt College, opened the panel with a detailed presentation of the scientific evidence that points to the reality of global warming and to the human contribution to those climatic changes. He highlighted the evidence that has led to an almost-universal consensus within the scientific community about global warming. This chapter is written in a style that makes the information quite accessible to nonscientists.

Kristen Page, a biology professor at Wheaton, followed with a message dear to the heart of God: what are the probable consequences of global climate change for humanity, especially for the poorest people in the world? As followers of Jesus Christ, who proclaimed good news to the poor, we are called to take decisive steps to love our poor neighbors—and future generations—as completely as possible.

P. J. Hill and Noah Toly then provided alternative responses to the climatic crisis. Hill urged Christians to make decisions that would take wise advantage of the international market economy to address present and future problems. Toly began by providing an analysis of the Kyoto Treaty. After pointing out the strengths and weaknesses of such intergovernmental treaties, he urged Christians to be supportive of wise governmental intervention through international accords. Taken together, these two presentations highlight the political and economic complexities of faithful response.

The second part of the volume includes examples of the ways that Wheaton College has attempted to respond to the multiple challenges of global warming and the care of creation. Sir John Houghton is one of the most eminent scientists in the world today. In 1988 he was influential in the formation of the Intergovernmental Panel on Climate Change (IPCC) and was appointed chairman of its scientific assessment—a position he held until 2002. The IPCC was recently the 2007 co-recipient of the Nobel Peace Prize for its arduous work in compiling massive studies on global warming and urging an equally massive response. What is not quite so well known is that Sir John is a dedicated follower of Jesus Christ. Sir John was invited to be the main speaker at the Evangelical Student Summit on Climate Change hosted on Wheaton's campus on January 23 and 24, 2007. In a period when controversies and conflicts between science and religion were heating up again, Sir John argued persuasively in his chapel talk, "Big Science, Big God," that the gigantic advances in science were not in conflict but in fact most compatible, with the big God of Christian Scriptures. You have in your hands not only his personal testimony but also his exhortation that followers of Jesus demonstrate their obedience to that big God through using the best of scientific knowledge.

The next two chapters come from Ben Lowe, who was president of the A Rocha chapter on Wheaton's campus during the 2006–2007 academic year. In his first chapter, "The Greening of Wheaton College: An Unlikely Tree Hugger," Ben describes the events that led him to a greater awareness of his responsibility as a Christian to care for creation and to love his worldwide neighbors through careful stewardship of the Earth's resources. In his second chapter, "The Greening of Wheaton College: A Bigger Vision," Ben describes what a small but committed group of students did to wake up an evangelical college to this God-given responsibility.

Vince Morris is the director of the Risk Management Office at Wheaton College. In 2005 President Litfin asked him to form and chair the Environmental Stewardship Advisory Committee. This group was charged with the tasks of 1) determining how Wheaton College is doing on creation care, 2) determining what "best practices" for creation care at Christian institutions might be, and 3) recommending changes to move the College from where we are to where we should be. In his chapter, Vince describes the small yet significant steps Wheaton has begun to take.

The epilogue was written by Professor Jeff Greenberg, for whom I am deeply grateful. He has taught geology at Wheaton for over two decades, and during 2007 played a key role in bringing creation care and global climate change to the forefront at Wheaton. In his chapter Jeff addresses this question, now that we are better informed about global warming, what should we do? His impassioned plea will inspire and challenge your mind and soul.

Special thanks go to two people who played key roles in bringing about this volume. Joy Trieglaff is the Program Coordinator of the Center for Applied Christian Ethics. She has literally "revolutionized" the entire ministry of the center. Jeremy Weber did a magnificent job of editing the presentations and making them available in a reader-friendly format. May this volume be used by God to wake us up and to stir us to loving action on behalf of our neighbors, as we take better care of his creation.

Lindy Scott

PART I

*A Panel Discussion
on Global Climate Change*

1 · INTRODUCTION TO THE PANEL DISCUSSION

A. Duane Litfin

I was asked to give a few introductory comments this evening for two reasons.

First, in my role as president of Wheaton College, I am often asked to speak an official word on behalf of the college. In this case, if you examine the College's confessional stance you will find an explicit affirmation of Wheaton's concern for our stewardship of God's creation. I want to affirm that the college takes seriously the issues of creation care.

But there is also a second, more personal reason I was asked to say a word: I am one of the original signatories of the widely published Evangelical Climate Initiative statement on global warming.

Some have asked why I signed that document. The answer: over the last two decades I have found within myself a growing awareness of and concern for these issues. I'm driven in this, as in so much else in my life, by my biblical and theological training and experience.

I am increasingly exercised about what it means to be a Christian living in the world today. How do we live in the light of a biblical understanding of God's created order, what happened to it through sin and brokenness, and the ways in which we continue in our sinfulness to defile this thing that God created good? What is our responsibility as his stewards of that created order, and how can we be a part of the redemptive process he initiated in Christ?

These sorts of theological issues drive me. As the awareness has dawned upon me as to what's happening with global climate change, particularly through human contributions, it has prompted me to become more and more concerned. So when I was asked to join that statement, I studied it carefully and decided to sign it.

I should point out that I do not often do that. Numerous causes come before me that people want me to sign onto. Yet I seldom add my name, even when I agree. The reason is, given my position, it's difficult for me to sign anything—that is, to stand up and put myself on the line for something—without taking Wheaton College with me.

That is in fact what has happened in this instance. No matter how hard I stress it, no matter how clearly I make the point that I'm signing this only as an individual, it seems to matter little. Because of my role as spokesperson for Wheaton College, it is in the nature of things that my signature is perceived as Duane Litfin putting Wheaton College on the line.

Because of that, once I signed the ECI statement, I began receiving a wide range of responses. Most of them, probably a large majority, have been affirming. But there have also been those who disagreed, raising questions as to whether I should be doing any such thing, precisely because of the inevitability of my taking the college with me. I have been reminded that whether I like it or not, I am perceived to be speaking for the entire Wheaton College community, and there may be voices in this community who are not well represented by what I was signing.

It's worth noting that I understand this concern. It goes hand in hand with leadership. Positions of leadership often empower you, but they also tend to muzzle you. It is enough for me to speak openly and forthrightly about things that have to do explicitly with the institution's stance. It's another thing for me to be signing my name to something that takes us beyond that, which, in some ways, the ECI statement does.

Yet I do not regret signing that statement. I am neither a scientist nor an economist, so I must be careful about making scientific or economic policy declarations. But my biblical and theological commitments tell me we need to stand up and be counted for the issues of neighbor care and creation care. We need to speak up.

But one of the results of my having joined the ECI statement is that I am far less naive about the range of opinions on this subject than when I started. Just this week I was struck by a *Newsweek* article wherein economist Robert Samuelson, a rather estimable voice, condemned the vaunted Stern Report as "a masterpiece of misleading public relations," one filled with "intellectual fictions" that will create the worst of both worlds; that is, a program that harms the economy without much helping the environment.[1]

---

1. Robert Samuelson, "The Worst of Both Worlds," *Newsweek*, November 13, 2006.

What are we nonscientists and non-economists to make of such disputes? The issues are daunting, and I have attempted to avoid dogmatism. But what I do know is that we are called to be faithful to the Lord in our stewardship of his creation. We see the facts of global warming; no one seems to be much debating that. The question is, what does it all mean? Is this warming generated by human beings? If so, how much of it? And if we can answer that question, what are we to do about it? What steps should we take, or what steps should we avoid? What does it all mean?

I know I am not the one to answer such questions. I'm here with you to learn. The issues are exceedingly complex and we should expect no simple answers. What we must do is listen to well-meaning, well-informed, even expert voices. And that is what we have the opportunity to do here tonight.

Let's listen together.

Accessed January 30, 2008. Online: http://www.newsweek.com/id/45565.

2 · IS THE SKY FALLING?
A BRIEF INTRODUCTION TO CLIMATE CHANGE SCIENCE

Douglas Allen

1. INTRODUCTION

Of potentially great importance to the future well-being of humankind is the threat of significant changes occurring in the Earth's "climate system": atmosphere, ocean, cryosphere (ice and snow), lithosphere (Earth's crust and outer mantle), and biosphere. Climate scientists have used various data sources to reconstruct past and presently evolving climate, while computer models are employed to predict future climate scenarios.

Various observations of the Earth's climate system have led to the consensus that the Earth's global average surface temperature has increased significantly over the last century (the so-called global warming). This warming may be due in part to natural climate forcings (volcanoes, solar variability), but human-caused factors likely play a significant (or even the major) role.

Of particular interest are the effects from increasing concentrations of greenhouse gases such as carbon dioxide, methane, and nitrous oxide, which absorb infrared radiation emitted from the Earth's surface and radiate a portion of it downward, thereby warming the surface. This "greenhouse effect" is crucial for maintaining habitable temperatures on the Earth. However, rising greenhouse gas concentrations above naturally occurring levels due to anthropogenic emissions may result in an "enhanced greenhouse effect," with serious climate consequences.

This chapter provides an overview of climate change science for a better understanding of the observations, models, and methodologies that climate scientists use to detect, attribute, and predict climate change.

2. WHY IS THE CLIMATE CHANGE DEBATE SO CONFUSING?

Before delving into the science of climate change, we need to first analyze the reasons why the climate change debate often seems so confusing.[1] This confusion is due to three types of problems: definitions and usage of the terms "weather" and "climate," various complications in the science of climate change, and philosophical biases of those presenting claims about climate change.

To help avoid problems with semantics, we first need some definitions. The Earth's climate and weather are both described in terms of the same physical properties of the atmosphere (temperature, wind, pressure, humidity, precipitation, and the like), which we'll refer to as climate variables. "Weather" refers to what is happening at any specific time. This statement, "Yesterday's high temperature in Wheaton, Illinois, was 56°F," is a statement about the weather. "Climate" refers to the average of the weather over time and/or geographic area. This statement, "The average high temperature in Wheaton on this date is 56°F," is a statement about climate, not weather.

"Climate change" refers to a change in the average value of a climate variable over a certain geographic area, while "global climate change" refers to the change in climate averaged over the whole Earth. Due to the nature of the averaging, the timescales of changes in climate (years to centuries) are much longer than typical changes in weather (minutes to days). A common error is to use a specific weather event (e.g., Hurricane Katrina) to implicate changes in climate. This can lead to confusion, since climate depends on the time-averaged weather, not on one specific event.

Besides confusion between the terms "weather" and "climate," there are several scientific reasons why the climate change debate can be confusing. First, climate changes occur on long timescales on the order of decades to centuries or longer, so we need long data records in order to discern trends. Analysis of long data records can often be complicated by missing data, changes in instrumentation or data-collection procedures, or biases among different data sets. These must be accounted for to avoid spurious climate trends.

---

1. For more details, see Andrew E. Dessler and Edward A. Parson, *The Science and Politics of Global Climate Change: A Guide to the Debate* (Cambridge: Cambridge University Press, 2006).

Second, climate changes are generally smaller than normal weather fluctuations. This means that scientists are trying to identify small trends underlying large fluctuations (i.e., small signal-to-noise ratio). This requires long, well-calibrated time series in order to obtain good statistics.

Third, the Earth's climate system is very complicated including numerous physical, chemical, and biotic processes. In order to fully analyze the complex interplay of these processes, sophisticated computer models are designed to build understanding of the climate system. Analyzing the model output often requires sophisticated mathematical operations (e.g., principal-component analysis) that are unfamiliar to the layperson.

Fourth, future projections depend on uncertain human actions, so climate researchers need to develop plausible scenarios about what humans are going to do, in order to have any confidence in forecasting climate. Finally, no one can be an expert in all areas of the debate. Even climate scientists, who are experts in certain areas, need to rely on their colleagues who are working in other areas. At some level, we all need to decide who we're going to trust.

There are also philosophical reasons why the climate change debate is confusing. First, worldviews influence how we filter scientific data. According to philosopher Roy Clouser, "Virtually all the major disagreements between rival theories in the sciences and in philosophy can be ultimately traced to the differences between the religious beliefs that guide them."[2] Religious beliefs, or worldviews, act as lenses through which we filter the scientific data. There is nothing inherently wrong with this, but we need to be honest about it as we approach this problem.

Second, rules of policy argument tend to be more lenient than rules of scientific argument. In policy argument, scientific "facts" are often twisted in order to support a particular position. The general public tends to be more forgiving about errors in policy argument than about errors in scientific argument. Third, policy debate demands fast answers and can be unsympathetic to scientific caution. Scientists tend to withhold conclusions until they are relatively certain, but policy decisions often cannot wait.

---

2. Roy A. Clouser, *The Myth of Religious Neutrality* (Notre Dame: University of Notre Dame Press, 2005), 3.

3. THE SCIENTIST'S ROLE IN THE CLIMATE CHANGE DEBATE

Given the complicating factors in the debate, one may wonder whether any headway can be made. In order to move forward, some guidelines are necessary to maintain integrity in the science amidst the many complicating factors.

For the purpose of this chapter, we want to address the question, what is the scientist's role in the climate change debate? The general responsibilities of climate scientists include providing accurate information about the likely magnitude, causes, impacts, and projections of global climate change. Scientists also have certain responsibilities to the public in terms of how they conduct their science and how they convey scientific information.

As discussed below, scientists should conduct their research using reliable time-tested tools, and they should convey the information by standard pathways of communication. The scientist must also be explicit about all assumptions that are being made, and levels of uncertainty and statistical significance should be provided. Scientists should present results that are reproducible and refutable, and the results should be quantitative, not merely anecdotal. Finally, claims that scientists make, whether in the published literature or in public statements, should whenever possible be referenced to peer-reviewed publications.

Among the tools available to climate scientists are direct and indirect observations of climate variables. Direct observations come from weather stations, ships, planes, buoys, and satellites. Indirect observations come from tree rings, ice cores, corals, ocean sediments, boreholes, and glacier records, among other naturally occurring phenomena.

These "proxy" measurements act like tape recorders of the climate. If scientists can show a strong correlation between the proxy variable and a climate variable when we have direct records, then they can project the climate variable back to times for which direct observations aren't available. For example, widths of tree rings have been shown to correlate well with the average global temperature over the last century or so.[3] We can then project backwards (using older trees) to estimate the temperature before regular measurements were available.

---

3. National Research Council, *Surface Temperature Reconstructions for the Last 2,000 Years* (Washington, DC: National Academies Press, 2006), 45–52.

To make sense of the observations, climate scientists build models of the Earth's climate system. Models take mathematical equations and put them into computer language to try to predict what climate variables are going to do. Global models cover the whole Earth, and regional models focus on limited areas. There are separate atmosphere and ocean models, as well as models that try to couple them together. These models vary tremendously in their complexity and scope. More details on models will be provided below.

How is the information produced by climate researchers disseminated to the general public? First, articles are published in peer-reviewed journals. When a scientist submits a paper for publication, it is received by an editor who relays it to peers within the field for review. The reviewers send the paper back to the editor with comments and an overall recommendation to publish, revise, or reject. This process acts as an effective (though not a perfect) filter to keep poor science out of the published literature.

These articles are scattered among dozens of different journals, so it is difficult for one individual to compile all the information. Scientific assessments are therefore performed in order to try to obtain a consensus view of a particular topic. The main assessments done in the area of climate science are published by the Intergovernmental Panel on Climate Change (IPCC). This panel involves collaboration among hundreds of scientists from dozens of nations in order to review the research to date and develop a consensus view. The IPCC has produced four reports, published in 1990, 1995, 2001, and 2007. This chapter will reference the *Third Assessment Report* (TAR)[4] and the *Fourth Assessment Report* (FAR).[5]

4. THE EVIDENCE FOR GLOBAL WARMING

One of the main questions climate scientists have focused on is whether the global average surface temperature is rising. What exactly is the "global average surface temperature"? If we could place a thermometer at

---

4. John T. Houghton, et al., eds., *Climate Change 2001: The Scientific Basis. Contributions of Working Group I to the Third Assessment Report of the Intergovernmental Panel on Climate Change* (Cambridge: Cambridge University Press, 2001).

5. Susan Solomon et al., eds., *Climate Change 2007: The Physical Science Basis: Contributions of Working Group I to the Fourth Assessment Report of the Intergovernmental Panel on Climate Change* (Cambridge: Cambridge University Press, 2007).

every location on the Earth's surface and average the temperature readings all taken at the same time, then the result would be considered a global average. Although thermometers aren't available at every location, weather stations, buoys, ship records, and remotely sensed satellite data provide a fairly good representative sampling. These data are averaged day and night over an entire year to obtain a single number, which represents the Earth's annual average temperature. After a number of years have been calculated, a plot can be made of how the average temperature changes over many years.

The IPCC Report of 2007 depicts the global annual average temperature from 1850 to 2005.[6] From 1850 to 1910, there was a slight warming phase followed by cooling, with the 1910 temperature returning to 1850s levels. From 1910 to 1940, the global average temperature increased linearly. From 1940 to 1970, the temperature leveled off or decreased slightly, and from 1970 to 2005, the temperature again increased linearly.

The overall picture shows a global average surface-temperature increase (or a "global warming") of 0.74°C (or about 1.3°F) over the last one hundred years.

"Well," you might say, "0.74°C doesn't sound like a lot. The weather can change by many degrees over a few hours or even minutes."

But here we're talking about a global, annual average temperature, for which 0.74°C is pretty large. It is estimated that during the last ice age the global average temperature was only around 5°C cooler than it is today.[7]

Therefore, we're seeing a pretty significant increase in terms of the global annual average. We can dissect this trend by isolating certain temporal or geographic locations. The warming is found to be larger over land than over oceans, larger at high latitudes than at low latitudes, and larger in the winter than in the summer.[8]

The temperature record can also be extended backwards in time using the proxy observations discussed earlier. One often-cited reconstruction is the Northern Hemisphere annual average temperature over the

6. Ibid.

7. James Hansen, "Diffusing the Global Warming Time Bomb," *Scientific American* 290 (2004) 68–77.

8. Solomon et al., eds., *Climate Change 2007: The Physical Science Basis: Contributions of Working Group I to the Fourth Assessment Report of the Intergovernmental Panel on Climate Change* (Cambridge: Cambridge University Press, 2007).

last millennium. There are several different versions of this reconstruction, based on a number of different proxies,[9] but they all show a general trend toward warmer temperatures around 1000 AD, the "Medieval Warm Period," followed by a general cooling for the next approximately 800 years, leading up to the "Little Ice Age" (circa 1500–1850).

Historical evidence supports the reconstructed temperatures. For example, the Medieval Warm Period is the time when Vikings settled Greenland, and the Little Ice Age is documented by historical records of very cold winters in northern Europe. The Little Ice Age is followed by the general warming trend observed since 1850. The thousand-year temperature plot has been called the "hockey-stick diagram," due to the shape of the gradual cooling followed by rapid warming. It seems to indicate that the warming over the last century is very unusual compared to the rest of the millennium.[10]

There are also other indicators of twentieth-century warming besides the global average temperature.[11] The sea level has risen approximately 17 cm over the last century, due to thermal expansion from warming waters and the flow of melted land ice into the ocean. The aerial coverage of Northern Hemisphere snow has declined. There has been widespread retreat of mountain glaciers.

The global ocean heat content has increased since the late 1950s (when we started collecting good data). There has been a 10 to 15 percent drop in Arctic spring and summer sea-ice extent. Observations from weather balloons and satellites have shown a warming of the lower and middle troposphere (the lower layer of the atmosphere, extending from the surface to about 10 km). And the average atmospheric water-vapor content has increased due to increased evaporation and the ability of warmer air to hold more water vapor.

---

9. National Research Council, *Surface Temperature Reconstructions for the Last 2,000 Years* (Washington DC: National Academies Press, 2006).

10. Michael E. Mann, R. S Bradley, and M. K. Hughes, "Northern Hemisphere Temperatures During the Past Millennium: Inferences, Uncertainties, and Limitations," *Geophysical Research Letters* 26 (1999) 759–62.

11. Solomon et al., eds., *Climate Change 2007: The Physical Science Basis: Contributions of Working Group I to the Fourth Assessment Report of the Intergovernmental Panel on Climate Change* (Cambridge: Cambridge University Press, 2007).

5. POTENTIAL NATURAL CAUSES OF TWENTIETH-CENTURY WARMING

The warming of the Earth's surface over the last century is very well documented, and strong scientific consensus exists that this has occurred. The obvious next step is to identify the cause of that warming. In the next two sections, we examine six different factors that play major roles in the Earth's climate history. In particular we will examine the plausibility of each factor in terms of the cause of the observed twentieth-century warming. Five of the factors are naturally occurring phenomena, while the sixth factor is anthropogenic (due to human activity).[12]

The first factor to be considered is variation in the Earth's orbit. The Earth orbits the Sun in an ellipse (not a circle), and the shape of that ellipse can change with time, due to the combined gravitational tug of the Sun, Moon, and other planets. The three main cyclical variations in the orbit are related to eccentricity (the shape of the ellipse), obliquity (the tilt of the Earth's axis), and precession (the time of year when the Earth is closest to the Sun). These variations are called "Milankovitch cycles," after the Serbian physicist that first proposed them.[13] These variations likely are the major contributor to the ice-age cycles in the Earth's climate history. However, the timescales of the changes are on the order of tens to hundreds of thousands of years—much too slow to account for the observed twentieth-century warming.

A second factor is the Earth's crust, composed of a number of different plates, which move relative to one another in a process called "plate tectonics." It is conceivable that a continent once at higher latitudes could move to tropical regions with much more direct sunlight; this move would dramatically change the continent's climate. However, the motion of these plates is rather lethargic, on the order of centimeters per year (approximately the rate at which your fingernails grow). So we can't use plate tectonics to explain the twentieth-century warming, because the associated timescales are far too long.

---

12. This section has benefited from arguments made in Dessler and Parson, *The Science and Politics of Global Climate Change: A Guide to the Debate* (Cambridge: Cambridge University Press, 2006).

13. W. S. Broecker and G. H. Denton, "What Drives Glacial Cycles?" *Scientific American* 262 (1990) 49–56.

What about volcanoes? Large eruptions throw significant amounts of material into the atmosphere that can dramatically alter climate. Besides large amounts of ash, volcanoes emit sulfur dioxide, which in the atmosphere converts into small aerosol particles that can scatter sunlight and cool the atmosphere. The year 1816 is often called "the year without a summer." The eruption of Mount Tambora in Indonesia ejected large amounts of material into the atmosphere, causing a widespread cooling. Snowstorms occurred as late as June in New England, and widespread crop failure occurred. It is clear that volcanoes can have a significant impact on climate, generally cooling the troposphere. However, their impact tends to decay over a few years, and explosive eruptions are episodic. Therefore it is unlikely that volcanoes caused the sustained global warming observed over the twentieth century.

What about internal variation of the atmosphere-ocean system? Natural cycles in this system such as El Niño and the North Atlantic Oscillation can result in significant regional (or local) impacts on weather. Their impacts can also extend over long distances through atmospheric teleconnections, in which weather patterns over widely separated regions are linked by large, coherent wavelike structures in the Earth's atmosphere. However, the magnitude of these observed changes tends to be too small to account for the observed global-scale warming, and the changes tend to happen in cycles rather than in long-term trends. It is therefore unlikely that internal variability accounts for the observed twentieth-century warming.

The last two factors provide the most promising answers. The first is solar variability. We know that solar variations have been strongly linked to variations in past climate. The total solar irradiance indicates the amount of energy from the Sun that hits the "top" of the Earth's atmosphere. The average power from solar energy reaching the Earth is approximately 1370 Watts per square meter (W/m2). Estimates of the past solar irradiance made using sunspot records (the number of sunspots has been correlated with total solar irradiance) have shown that in the late 1600s the solar output was approximately 0.25 percent less than it is today.[14] This coincided with the coldest period of the Little Ice Age, implicating solar variability as a major factor in that climate episode.

---

14. Judith Lean et al., "SORCE Contributions to New Understanding of Global Change and Solar Variability," *Solar Physics* 230 (2005) 27–53.

It is difficult to precisely measure the solar irradiance from the Earth's surface, however, since the gases, dust, and clouds in the atmosphere scatter and absorb some of the Sun's radiation. The best estimates of irradiance have occurred only since 1979, when solar monitoring instruments were installed on Earth-orbiting satellites, far above the Earth's obscuring atmosphere. The data taken since 1979 show that there may have been a slight increase (less than 1 W/m2) in solar irradiance over the last twenty-five years,[15] which may account for a small part of the observed warming over the last few decades but not for the bulk of the warming.

Theories speculate about how solar variations may affect the Earth's climate, apart from the direct forcing due to changes in solar irradiance. A controversial theory originally proposed in 1997 by Svensmark and Friis-Christensen argues that changes in the solar magnetic field alter the amount of galactic cosmic rays entering the Earth's atmosphere.[16] These cosmic rays may affect the amount of cloud cover and thereby change the amount of light reflected from the Earth's atmosphere. This effect could amplify the Sun's influence on Earth's climate. However, many climate scientists are skeptical that this mechanism plays a major role in global warming.

6. POTENTIAL ANTHROPOGENIC CAUSES OF TWENTIETH-CENTURY WARMING

After examining potential natural causes of twentieth-century warming, we now turn to the final, promising factor: anthropogenic causes. The main way humans can impact climate is through emissions of gases and particles into the air that alter the energy flow in the Earth's atmosphere. As we will see, the human impact may either cool or warm the Earth depending on a number of factors. To understand the human impact, we first need to explain the greenhouse effect.

The Sun, at a temperature of around 6000°C, radiates most of its energy in the visible and ultraviolet (UV) portions of the electromagnetic spectrum. This radiant energy travels 150 million kilometers through ba-

---

15. Judith Lean, "Living with a Variable Sun," *Physics Today* 58 (2005) 32–38.

16. H. Svensmark, and E. Friis-Christensen, "Variation of Cosmic-Ray Flux and Global Cloud Coverage—a Missing Link in Solar-Climate Relationships," *Journal of Atmospheric and Solar-Terrestrial Physics* 59 (1997) 1225–32.

sically empty space before it reaches the Earth's upper atmosphere. The atmosphere is mostly transparent to visible light, which is nice so that we can see the Sun, Moon, stars, and so forth. Some of the visible light is reflected back to space by clouds and shiny surfaces like ice and snow, and some is scattered away by the gases and particles in the atmosphere. On average, about 70 percent of the incoming sunlight is absorbed by the Earth's surface. This causes the surface to warm and become a radiator itself. The Earth's average temperature is much lower (about 15°C), so it radiates mainly in the infrared region rather than visible and UV rays.

The atmosphere is much less transparent to infrared energy, due to greenhouses gases. If those gases were not in the atmosphere, the infrared radiation from the surface would go directly back to space. Simple calculations show that the Earth's average surface temperature would then be about -6°C (about 21°F), which would make for a much less comfortable planet![17] The greenhouse gases absorb outgoing infrared radiation and send some of it back toward the surface, acting like a blanket to trap some heat in and keep the surface temperature warmer. With the greenhouse gases, the Earth's average temperature is around +15°C (about 59°F), a much more comfortable level.

We find from these calculations that the greenhouse effect is essential for life on this planet. What we're concerned about is the thickening of the greenhouse "blanket" caused by human emissions of heat-trapping gases, which make for an enhanced greenhouse effect. Thickening the blanket will trap more infrared energy and could cause an undesired warming of the Earth's surface.

What are the greenhouse gases? First, we note that water vapor is actually the dominant greenhouse gas, absorbing the most infrared energy. But water-vapor amount responds quickly to the atmospheric temperature, and thus is treated as a part of the climate system that responds to external forcing rather than as a forcing agent itself.

Carbon dioxide, methane, and nitrous oxide are the three most important greenhouse gases, while minor greenhouse gases include chlorofluorocarbons (CFCs), hydrofluorocarbons (HCFCs), and tropospheric ozone. Each of the major greenhouse gases has both natural and anthropogenic sources. Carbon dioxide is produced by respiration and plant

---

17. John T. Houghton, *Global Warming: The Complete Briefing*, 3d ed. (Cambridge: Cambridge University Press, 2004).

decomposition as well as by fossil fuel burning and biomass burning (for example, by clearing forests). Methane is produced by ruminant animals and wetlands as well as by rice paddies, biomass burning, landfills, and natural gas exploitation. Nitrous oxide is produced by natural soil processes as well as by fossil fuel burning and fertilizer application.

It is important to emphasize that the effects of putting these gases into the atmosphere extend over long time periods. Although residence timescales in the atmosphere vary for these gases, it is estimated that the average residence times are on the order of decades to a century or more.[18] Once in the atmosphere, these gases can affect the climate well into the future.

Have greenhouse gas concentrations been increasing over the last century? The answer is an unequivocal yes. Since the industrial revolution (around 1750), carbon dioxide has increased from 280 parts per million (i.e., molecules of carbon dioxide compared with molecules of air) to 379 parts per million in 2005, an increase of 35 percent. In addition, nitrous oxide has risen by 18 percent, and methane has risen by over 140 percent since the industrial revolution.[19]

When fossil fuels are burned, they give off more than just greenhouse gases. One important by-product of coal combustion is sulfur dioxide. Once in the atmosphere, sulfur dioxide reacts chemically with air to produce sulfate aerosols, which tend to cool the atmosphere both directly (by scattering sunlight) and indirectly (by serving as condensation nuclei for small cloud particles and so producing what is known as the indirect aerosol effect). This cooling somewhat offsets the warming from greenhouse gases. As we will see, sulfate aerosols likely played a major role in the global average cooling trend observed from 1940 to 1970.

When we compare trends in greenhouse gas concentration and global average surface temperature, we find a good correlation, particularly over the last few decades. We might argue that the case is closed: the increased greenhouse gases must have caused the global warming. However, correlation does not by itself indicate cause and effect. As a trivial example, suppose you observed a rooster crowing every morning just before the sun rose. There is a clear correlation, but you wouldn't

18. Solomon et al., eds., *Climate Change 2007: The Scientific Basis. Contributions of Working Group I to the Fourth Assessment Report of the Intergovernmental Panel on Climate Change*, 2007.

19. Ibid.

argue that the rooster's crow caused the sun to rise. In the case of climate change, we need to develop physical models to test whether the warming is actually due to the increased greenhouse gases or to something else.

7. CLIMATE MODELS

In order to attribute changes in climate to particular forcing mechanisms, climate scientists develop computer models to try to determine and quantify the causal relationships. These models attempt to incorporate all the important processes of the Earth's climate system, including changes in solar input, sea ice, volcanoes, precipitation, and land use.

Climate models are similar to weather models, which also need to include the most important physical processes. However, weather models are used to make short-term forecasts of climate variables (forecasts of days or weeks), whereas climate models are used to develop long-term averages (averages for years to centuries). Climate models are first used to reconstruct the past climate record. Once we understand the past climate, then the models can be used to project climate into the future.

Since the Earth's climate system is so complex, with many interacting factors, scientists often like to start with very simple models, isolating each individual factor affecting the Earth's climate apart from all other factors. The change in the amount of energy retained at the Earth's surface due to changes in a given factor is called the "radiative forcing."

The latest IPCC report presents the radiative forcing to the climate system for 2005 relative to the year 1750. For example, the carbon-dioxide increase since 1750 is expected to cause an increased forcing of 1.6 Watts per square meter of the Earth. Combined with the other greenhouse gas increases, there is a total of around 3 W/m2 of forcing. By comparison, the radiative forcing from the direct effect of solar irradiance alone is found to be much smaller, around 0.1 W/m2.

Other factors exist, such as the sulfates and other aerosols, that provide a negative forcing (i.e., cooling) of the atmosphere. There is still quite a bit of uncertainty in quantifying the radiative forcing due to aerosols, but clearly a negative forcing serves to offset the warming from increased greenhouse gases.

Most of us don't deal with watts per square meter, but we do understand temperature. So the next problem is how to translate the forcing components into temperature. The simplest climate model of the

Earth-Sun system is composed of an equation that balances solar energy absorbed by the Earth's surface with the infrared energy radiated by the Earth. If we assume no greenhouse gases or clouds, the Earth's surface should absorb around 84 percent of the incoming solar energy. The outgoing radiation from the Earth depends only on its temperature (proportional to temperature to the fourth power). Equating the two quantities (absorbed energy and radiated energy) results in an average temperature of -6°C (15°F), the number we quoted earlier. Including greenhouse gases (and clouds) results in the observed average temperature of 15°C (59°F). Now if we double the carbon-dioxide concentration, keeping all other factors constant, projections indicate carbon dioxide will likely double by the year 2100. Our simple model shows that this change alone will result in a temperature increase of about 1.2°C.[20]

However, changes in the atmosphere are not isolated, but are further modified by other changes, called feedbacks. For example, suppose carbon-dioxide increases begin to warm the Earth's surface. This warming should cause increased evaporation, leading to increased water vapor. This in turn warms the surface further, since water vapor is a greenhouse gas. This would be an example of a positive feedback. Another positive feedback is that warmer temperatures should cause melting of ice and snow. This would make the Earth less reflective, allowing the surface to absorb more energy and thereby further warming the surface. Negative feedbacks exist that could counter changes to one component in the system.

Taking account of all the feedbacks involves more sophisticated models, which vary somewhat in their conclusions. However, the models generally predict an amplification of the carbon-dioxide–doubling effect from positive feedbacks, resulting in a temperature increase between 2 and 4.5°C. This provides a ballpark estimate of how we might expect the climate system to change due to a doubling of carbon dioxide.

Now we want to build a more complex model, incorporating all known physical properties, to obtain more accurate projections of the Earth's future climate. Dozens of models have been developed at numerous research institutions worldwide to try to reconstruct past climate and predict climate into the future. The nice thing about having a complete

---

20. John T. Houghton, *Global Warming: The Complete Briefing*, 3d ed. (Cambridge: Cambridge University Press, 2004).

model is that you can do various "experiments" with the model by changing various forcing parameters. For example, model reconstructions by Stott and coworkers have been used to reproduce the Earth's global average surface temperature from 1860 to 2000.[21] In certain model runs, only natural forcings (solar, volcanic, and the like) are used, while in other runs, only anthropogenic forcing (increased greenhouse gases and aerosols) is used. In a third set of runs, all forcings (natural and anthropogenic) are used. Simulations using natural forcings alone do not capture the sharp warming from 1970 to 2000. Simulations using anthropogenic forcings alone do not capture the warming from 1910 to 1940. The results of these simulations show that in a reliable reconstruction of the past 150 years, both natural and anthropogenic forcings need to be included.

Detailed analysis of the model data shows that the 1910–1940 warming was likely caused mainly by increases in solar irradiance (combined with a lack of major volcanic activity during this period), while the cooling from 1940 to 1970 was largely caused by increased sulfate aerosol concentrations. The warming from 1970 to 2000 was found to be almost certainly due to increases in greenhouse gases. Other modeling results have corroborated the main conclusions of the work by Stott and co-workers, but several quantitative details still need to be resolved.

Having obtained reliable reconstructions of the past 150 years, climate modelers have built confidence in projecting the models into the future. To do a projection is to make some assumptions about what humans will do in the future. The IPCC has developed a number of different scenarios, which take into account changes in energy use, technology, population growth, and other factors. Modelers run projections for a number of different scenarios in order to obtain a range of possible results. The IPCC reports have documented projections out to the year 2100 from a number of different models and several different scenarios.

The general result is that all models show a projected warming, with the amount of warming varying between around 1.1 and 6.4°C. This is broadly consistent with the simple estimates based on doubled carbon dioxide. The models also generally predict increased precipitation and a sea-level rise of around 18 to 59 cm. There is still a lot of uncertainty in precisely how much the temperature and sea level will rise, but there

---

21. Peter A. Stott et al., "External Control of 20th Century Temperature by Natural and Anthropogenic Forcings," *Science* 290 (2000) 2133–37.

is strong evidence that warming and rising of significant magnitude will occur.

8. CONSEQUENCES

What are some of the consequences of this projected global warming, and how sure are we of these consequences?[22] Over the next century, several changes are virtually certain to happen. First, due to increased energy consumption and long residence time of greenhouse gases, it is virtually certain that greenhouse gas concentrations will continue to rise for quite a long time (several centuries). It is also virtually certain that the temperatures will continue to rise throughout the twenty-first century. This temperature rise will result in melting ice, retreating glaciers, and rising sea levels. The higher sea levels will make coastlines more vulnerable to erosion and will threaten low-lying islands.

On other possible consequences of global warming, the consensus among scientists is not quite as strong. Increased ocean temperatures will potentially fuel stronger and more frequent tropical storms (hurricanes and tsunamis). This is an area of active research and much debate, in which scientific consensus has not yet been reached. Intensifying heat waves are possible, as well as worsening droughts. Warmer air can cause more soil evaporation, which can exacerbate the warmer temperatures. Increased flooding may also occur in certain regions. In addition, diseases that have generally been confined to the tropical regions could possibly migrate to higher latitudes. Proliferating tornadoes are unlikely, since the physics of tornado development is not directly related to large-scale temperature increases.

Predicting changes for a particular region is more difficult than predicting changes on the global scale. The largest warming is projected to occur in the Arctic region, with milder warming occurring at lower latitudes. Continents are expected to warm more rapidly than oceans. Patterns of precipitation will likely change, and ice cover and snow cover will continue to decrease. Some regions may actually benefit (at least

22. John A. Knox, "Living in a Globally Warmed World," *Phi Kappa Phi Forum* 86 (2006) 11–16. See also Solomon et al., eds. *Climate Change 2007: The Physical Science Basis. Contributions of Working Group I to the Fourth Assessment Report of the Intergovernmental Panel on Climate Change* (Cambridge: Cambridge University Press, 2007).

temporarily) from longer growing seasons and increased precipitation, while other regions may suffer from increased drought and heat waves. In general, the poorest nations are more vulnerable to climate changes since they have fewer resources for adaptation.

9. SUMMARY

In summary, many complex factors influence climate. Some we understand well, while others are poorly understood. Observational evidence supports global average surface warming of 0.74°C, a sea-level rise of 17 cm over the last century, and widespread melting of snow and ice. Most of the observed increase in globally averaged temperatures since the mid-twentieth century is very likely due to the observed increase in anthropogenic greenhouse gas concentrations.

Climate models project additional warming of 1.1 to 6.4°C and a sea-level rise of 18 to 59 cm by end of the twenty-first century. Other global-scale impacts are projected to occur, with varying degrees of certainty. Regional impacts are also likely, but specific projections of these are more uncertain than large-scale projections.

BIBLIOGRAPHY

Broecker R. S., and G. H. Denton. "What Drives Glacial Cycles?" *Scientific American* 262 (1990) 49–56.

Clouser, Roy. *The Myth of Religious Neutrality: An Essay on the Hidden Role of Religious Belief in Theories*. Revised ed. Notre Dame: University of Notre Dame Press, 2005.

Dessler, Andrew E., and Edward A. Parson. *The Science and Politics of Global Climate Change: A Guide to the Debate*. Cambridge: Cambridge University Press, 2006.

Hansen, James. "Diffusing the Global Warming Time Bomb." *Scientific American* 290 (2004) 68–77.

Houghton, John T. *Global Warming: The Complete Briefing*. 3d edition. Cambridge: Cambridge University Press, 2004.

Houghton, John T. et al., editors. *Climate Change 2001: The Scientific Basis. Contribution of Working Group I to the Third Assessment Report of the Intergovernmental Panel on Climate Change*. Cambridge: Cambridge University Press, 2001.

Knox, John. "Living in a Globally Warmed World." *Phi Kappa Phi Forum* 86 (2006) 11–16.

Lean, Judith G. "Living with a Variable Sun." *Physics Today* 58 (2005) 32–38.

Lean. Judith G., et al. "SORCE Contributions to New Understanding of Global Change and Solar Variability." *Solar Physics* 230 (2005) 27–53.

Mann, Michael E., R. S. Bradley, and M. K. Hughes. "Northern Hemisphere Temperatures During the Past Millennium: Inferences, Uncertainties, and Limitations." *Geophysical Research Letters* 26 (1999) 759–62.

National Research Council of the National Academies. *Surface Temperature Reconstructions for the Last 2,000 Years*. Washington DC: National Academies Press, 2006.

Solomon, Susan, et al., editors. *Climate Change 2007: The Physical Science Basis. Contributions of Working Group I to the Fourth Assessment Report of the Intergovernmental Panel on Climate Change*. Cambridge: Cambridge University Press, 2007.

Stott Peter A., et al. "External Control of 20th Century Temperature by Natural and Anthropogenic Forcings." *Science* 290 (2000) 2133–37.

Svensmark, H., and E. Friis-Christensen. "Variation of Cosmic-Ray Flux and Global Cloud Coverage—A Missing Link in Solar-Climate Relationships." *Journal of Atmospheric and Solar-Terrestrial Physics* 59 (1997) 1225–32.

3 · GLOBAL CLIMATE: IMPLICATIONS FOR GLOBAL HEALTH

L. Kristen Page

INTRODUCTION

Human health is intricately associated with ecosystem function. Our well-being depends on many ecosystem functions, including food production, water filtration, seed dispersal, pollination, drought and flood mitigation, disease regulation, and carbon storage.[1] Often these services are overlooked until overuse of resources, pollution, or other stressors cause failures resulting in economic losses or changes in human health.

The process of global warming necessarily alters ecosystem processes,[2] and thus alters ecosystem services directly and indirectly related to human health.[3] The objective of this chapter is to discuss the implications of a warming climate on human health. We will examine climatic factors that directly impact human health (i.e., extreme weather events), ecosystem-mediated factors that impact disease transmission and food production, and finally indirect effects such as population displacement as a result of climate change (e.g., rising sea level).

Before we can begin this discussion, it is necessary to overview the current state of human health irrespective of climate. Disease affects different human populations in different ways. People in less-developed countries rarely have the infrastructure to respond adequately to disease and its effects. Many live in tropical ecosystems with more naturally oc-

---

1. Corvalán et al. 2005.

2. Strong scientific consensus exists that global temperatures are warming, and this chapter is written from that perspective. The United Nations Environmental Program and the World Meteorological Organization established the Intergovernmental Panel on Climate Change in 1988. IPCC 2007, McMichael et al. 2006.

3. As ecosystems are degraded, land becomes less productive, leading to increased incidence of malnutrition; or vector habitat increases, leading to increased transmission of vectorborne disease.

curring pathogens and vectors (such as mosquitoes) that transmit disease, and people are often living at such high densities that disease moves quickly from person to person. Currently millions of people worldwide die yearly of preventable diseases. An estimated 80 percent of the world's population lives in the developing countries, and approximately 1.2 billion people live on less than one dollar per day.[4]

An examination of the prevalence of disease on a global scale demonstrates that the poor of the world are not only sicker than the affluent,[5] but they are also more frequently exposed to disease and less likely to have access to medical services.[6] In much the same way, climate change also will disproportionately affect the Global South, as already-vulnerable populations may experience an increased frequency of extreme weather events, increased sea levels, changes in productivity,[7] and increased exposure to arthropod disease vectors.[8]

CLIMATE AND HEALTH: AN OVERVIEW

Overwhelming scientific consensus exists that global climate change is occurring, and that human actions are a driving force in the increase of greenhouse gases.[9] The relationship between these changes and human health are difficult to quantify directly; however, it is not disputed that climate change will affect human health,[10] In fact, current trends in emerging infectious diseases can already be linked to increasing global temperatures and extreme weather events,[11] and mounting ecological and epidemiological evidence allows scientists to predict with accuracy the human populations at greatest risk for changes in health status.

Human alteration of ecosystems and changes in interactions between humans and the environment are the most commonly recognized factors

---

4. Boff 1997.
5. Farmer 2003.
6. Farmer 1999.
7. "Productivity" in this sense refers to plant production that ultimately affects the entire food chain.
8. IPCC 2007.
9. IPCC 2007, Oreskes 2004.
10. McMichael et al. 2006, IPCC 2007, Corvalán et al. 2005.
11. Corvalán et al. 2005, Patz et al. 2003.

contributing to the emergence of disease.[12] Activities such as deforestation, irrigation, dam building, wetland modification, and agriculture can result in very specific ecological changes that enhance the transmission of diseases.[13]

Increased human pressures on the environment manifest in climate changes have direct, ecosystem-mediated, and indirect impacts on human health.[14] Direct impacts on human health include problems associated with flooding, extreme temperatures, drought, and landslides associated with extreme precipitation events and erosion. Ecosystem-mediated effects include emerging infectious diseases associated with changes in vector populations or water temperatures, and loss of natural disease reservoirs or of botanical medicines from loss of biodiversity. Climate change can also indirectly affect health, as changes in distribution of agriculturally productive land result in livelihood loss, malnutrition, and population displacement.[15]

CLIMATE AND DIRECT IMPACTS ON HUMAN HEALTH

Certain effects of climate change on human health are directly observable. Extreme weather events, flooding, drought, and landslides can result in predictable and measurable health problems. The IPCC suggests that as global temperatures rise, extreme weather events (such as intensifying heat waves) are very likely.[16]

Such events have direct effects on human health, though the effects are highly variable across latitudinal gradients. Populations acclimated to higher temperatures are more vulnerable to extreme cold, and populations in cooler climates are more vulnerable to extreme heat. Even within populations, certain individuals (the elderly, the homeless, and the infirm) are at greater risk of succumbing to intense heat or extreme cold. Heat-wave deaths are frequent among individuals with preexisting

---

12. Morse 1995.
13. Patz et al. 2004, Slingenbergh et al. 2004.
14. Corvalán et al. 2005.
15. Corvalán et al. 2005, McMichael et al. 2006.
16. The IPCC 2007 report uses the following terminology and associated probability of occurrence: virtually certain (>99% probability of occurrence), very likely (90–99%), likely (66–90%), about as likely as not (22–66%), unlikely (10–33%), very unlikely (1–10%), and exceptionally unlikely (<1%).

cardiovascular or respiratory diseases.[17] The 2003 heat wave in Europe resulted in thirty thousand deaths and demonstrated the devastation associated with such events.[18]

The IPCC considers likely the increased frequency of other extreme weather events such as flooding and droughts;[19] however, certain health risks are associated with these events. Flooding initially results in traumatic injury and ultimately can result in outbreaks of bacterial diseases associated with the failure of septic systems, with reactions to mold, and with the ultimate spread of contaminated water into living spaces.[20] The loss of lives in flooded regions following the 2004 Indonesian tsunami[21] and Hurricane Katrina in 2005[22] is a sobering reminder of the devastation linked with the initial storm. However, the subsequent loss of life from bacterial diseases (cholera, salmonella, and the like) for extended periods following the initial storms demonstrate the far-reaching effects of a single extreme weather event.

The frequency and extent of droughts over the past decade have increased for certain tropical regions. According to the IPCC, the land area affected by droughts likely will continue to increase. Direct effects of drought on human health include lack of water, water contamination, and subsequent increases in waterborne disease. In addition, food production is decreased due to land degradation.

Though the land area affected by drought may be relatively small, a significant number of people live in these drought-prone areas; thus a single drought event could be devastating. For example, the 1990–1991 drought in southern Africa put forty million people at risk of starvation.[23] A rapid response by the World Health Organization (WHO) and other relief agencies prevented many deaths; however, if drought increases in frequency and land-area, resources for such a relief response may become strained.

17. McMichael et al. 2006.
18. McMichael et al. 2006, Knox 2006.
19. Also see Knox 2006 for a summary of probabilities associated with specific changes in global climate.
20. McMichael 2006.
21. Morgan et al. 2005.
22. Wilson 2006
23. WHO 2004.

Currently malnutrition accounts for 10 percent of the global disease burden, irrespective of projected changes in climate. Thus as land continues to experience degradation and as droughts increase in frequency, we can expect increases in global disease. In addition to malnutrition, drought has other effects on health. Mosquito-borne disease often increases as rains follow a drought,[24] and fires in drought-prone regions decrease air quality, thus increasing the frequency of respiratory diseases.

CLIMATE AND ECOSYSTEM-MEDIATED EFFECTS ON HUMAN HEALTH

The relationship between climate and seasonal emergence of disease has been understood for centuries. Roman aristocrats anticipated the seasonal emergence of malaria and retreated to homes in the hills during the summer. Strongly curried foods became common cuisine for some South Asian peoples during the hottest part of summer, when foods were more susceptible to bacterial contamination.[25] And the Navajo elders of the Colorado Plateau recognized that in years following heavy spring rains (in El Niño years), the mouse (*Na'ats'oosi*) would bring a sickness (*ch'osh dooyet'iinii*) to the young Navajo (hantavirus).[26] Ecological and epidemiological studies have confirmed this previously observed link between climate events and health, and models allow for accurate predictions of disease emergence.[27]

Disease transmission is dependent on host-population dynamics (which are often impacted by weather events) and on other ecological factors. Pathogens and host populations change (they grow or decline) as a function of temperature or precipitation. For example, the 1993 emergence of hantavirus pulmonary syndrome (HPS) followed an El Niño year. Rains on the Colorado Plateau increased the productivity of plants, and resulted in a bumper crop of seeds. The following spring, mouse populations increased due to an increase in available food. As a result, humans were more likely to come into contact with mice (and

---

24. Ibid.
25. Patz et al. 2003
26. Walters 2003.
27. WHO 2004.

their urine); such contact led to an outbreak of HPS.[28] This example of ecosystem-mediated effects of climate on human health illustrates the complexity of ecological relationships that if perturbed can result in changes in disease transmission.

Most of the ecosystem-mediated responses can be linked to increasing global temperatures (surface and ocean temperatures). Global surface temperatures have increased 0.74°C over the past one hundred years,[29] and ocean temperatures are rising as well.[30] But the effects of increased surface temperatures are not all negative. In fact, at higher latitudes increased growing seasons may actually increase food production. However, with increased plant productivity, an increase in aeroallergen problems should be expected.[31] While food production might increase for some regions, the majority of the world is expected to experience increased health risks associated with rising surface temperatures. Ecological and epidemiological evidence currently demonstrates expanded ranges for arthropod vectors of disease (primarily mosquitoes) and for diarrhea-causing pathogens.

Vectorborne diseases demonstrate seasonal patterns because vectors have measurable responses to changes in temperature and precipitation. Vector survival, reproduction, and range can increase as temperatures increase in northern latitudes or at higher altitudes,[32] and as precipitation increases, more vector habitat becomes available. Vectorborne pathogens also respond to increases in temperatures, often altering the transmission season, distribution, and replication.[33]

Malaria is a preventable and treatable mosquito-vectored disease. Forty percent of the global population is currently at risk of acquiring malaria; five hundred million people per year are diagnosed with the

28. Glass et al. 2000.

29. See Douglas Allen's chapter for an explanation of climate data and accepted interpretations.

30. The consensus is not as strong for ocean temperature rise; however, the IPCC 2007 report states with high confidence (an eight-out-of-ten chance) that changes in marine systems are related to a rise in ocean temperatures.

31. McMichael et al. 2006.

32. Vector biology is highly species specific, but in general warmer temperatures facilitate reproduction and range-expansion.

33. Patz et al. 2003.

disease, and one million per year die (primarily children).[34] Though this disease is preventable, most of the people living in endemic regions do not have access to mosquito nets, medicines, or other means of protection and treatment often available to people in developed countries.

Populations at greatest risk of severe complications with malaria are those populations that are on the edge of the spreading range of the mosquito vectors. Populations that have no previous exposure to malaria, and thus no acquired immunity, are at great risk of epidemic emergences of malaria. As global temperatures rise, mosquito ranges are expected to expand, and epidemics have been reported at high-altitude locations previously not expected to be suitable for the vector,[35] Other mosquito-borne diseases that are expected to expand in range and increase in epidemic frequency are yellow fever, dengue hemorrhagic fever, Japanese encephalitis, St. Louis encephalitis, and West Nile virus.

Bacterial pathogens proliferate in warm temperatures and are expected to become more problematic as surface and ocean temperatures continue to rise. There is a well-documented link between cholera epidemics and climate.

Cholera is a bacterial infection acquired via the ingestion of contaminated food or water. Infections result in severe diarrhea and can be fatal within days if treatment for dehydration is not received. Cholera is pandemic and exhibits seasonal emergences associated with warming ocean currents such as with El Niño events.[36] The cholera bacterium proliferates on plankton particles,[37] and the bacteria often reach a high enough abundance that a single plankton particle is infective to a person. Warming waters enhance the growth of phytoplankton and zooplankton, thus increasing the available substrate for cholera to reproduce.

Cholera typically emerges in poorly developed regions, where there is little access to sanitation, and emergences can have devastating effects on the health of such regions. For example, between April 21 and June

---

34. WHO malaria fact sheet.
35. Shanks et al. 2002 Checchi et al. 2006.
36. Long et al. 2005.

37. *Plankton* is a term that describes free-floating particles. Frequently these particles are algal/plant (phytoplankton) or animal (zooplankton). Cholera bacteria attaches to phyto- or zooplankton in order to reproduce.

18, 2006, there were over 2000 cases and 77 deaths caused by a cholera epidemic in Northern Sudan.[38]

Warming surface and oceanic temperatures have further implications for human health due to impacts on ecological processes beyond those involved in disease transmission. Temperature plays an important role in seasonal plant cycles and photosynthesis (productivity). The IPCC assigns very high confidence to a probable shift in timing of spring events, and to expansion of species ranges to northern latitudes. If timing of flowering does not correspond to timing of migration of pollinators, there could be significant failures in food production.[39]

Plant productivity can increase as temperatures rise;[40] however, there is a point when increased productivity can be detrimental to aquatic ecosystems. As plant productivity increases, organisms that break down plant material consume oxygen until the environment becomes anoxic.[41] At this point, oxygen-dependent organisms that feed higher on the food chain are lost. Because photosynthesis provides the energy at the base of the food chain, anything that affects productivity can ultimately affect feeding relationships all along the chain. Shifts in productivity and ranges of algae and phytoplankton have been implicated in fishery declines and subsequent food shortages.

CLIMATE AND INDIRECT IMPACTS ON HUMAN HEALTH

Indirect effects of climate change on health are necessarily related to direct and ecosystem-mediated effects; however, this category is referring specifically to the indirect effects of population displacement as a result of direct and ecosystem-mediated impacts.

---

38. WHO Epidemic and Pandemic Alert and Response: http://www.who.int/csr/don/2006_06_21a/en/index.html.

39. This phenomenon applies to both domesticated crops and natural food sources (e.g., seeds). Shifts in availability of natural food sources will have an effect on many bird and mammal populations that serve as reservoirs of disease. As seeds increase in abundance, vertebrate reservoirs increase in numbers. In addition, domestic food production depends on natural pollinators; therefore, shifts in flowering time could ultimately have an effect on food production.

40. The relationship between photosynthesis and temperature is species dependent. Some species are much more tolerant to changes in temperature than other species.

41. This process is termed *eutrophication*.

Climate change indirectly affects health when populations are displaced due to changes in distribution of agriculturally productive land, and often results in malnutrition and other infectious diseases. Population displacement has many causes, both social causes (e.g., conflict) and ecological causes. Many of the climate-related causes have already been discussed: extreme weather events such as flooding and drought, and changes in agricultural productivity.

Sea-level rise is another climate event that will displace significant numbers of people. The extent of expected sea-level rise is disputed;[42] however if it occurs, it will affect some of the poorest and highest-density populations of the world. The IPCC 2007 report states that sea-level rise is likely, and that results will include salinization of irrigation water, decreased freshwater availability, increased risk of drowning death, and significant migration-related health risks.

The 2004 Indonesian tsunami affected two billion people and displaced one million.[43] Displaced populations are at increased risk of bacterial infections (e.g., cholera, salmonella), of protein-energy malnutrition,[44] of dehydration from lack of clean water, and of traumatic injury. In 2005, eleven million refugees were displaced, most of whom were women.[45] Women's health is further compromised due to the increased likelihood of poverty and hence of sexual violence, exploitation, and trafficking.

Beyond the immediate health concerns arising from climate change, associated environmental changes may also lead to emotional distress and depression. As climate changes result in more-frequent extreme weather events, changes in food production, and possibly sea-level rise, more populations will become displaced. This will result in significant changes in the global burden of disease.

OUR RESPONSE

The debate over climate change has spanned nearly two decades. The United Nations Environmental Program and the World Meteorological Organization established the IPCC in 1988, at a time when the annual

---

42. Knox 2006.
43. UNFPA 2005.
44. Protein-energy malnutrition is one of the leading causes of childhood mortality.
45. UNFPA 2005.

global temperature was rising sharply. This panel has published reports in 1992, 1996, 2001, 2003, and 2007. Each report, based on a steadily increasing body of scientific literature, made suggestions to policymakers and scientists about setting priorities for a response.

Currently it is rarely debated that climate is changing; however, the argument over cause and appropriate response continues.[46] Arguments about the degree of anthropogenic contributions to greenhouse gas emissions continue to slow any response to increasing global temperatures. The link between greenhouse gases and climate change is established, so why should we wait to settle the argument before we start to act?

Regardless of blame, it is within our power to respond to increasing global temperatures. We can change our patterns of consumption and can reduce our emissions. The smallest proportion of the global population accrues the most wealth, consumes the most resources, and contributes the most to greenhouse gas emissions. As the affluent continue to increase their use of natural resources and concurrently to increase their contributions to global waste, the poor continue to struggle. Due to globalization, consumption rates have increased even in some developing countries. Certainly everyone will need to reduce consumption patterns; however, the affluent have the capacity to make the greatest change in resource use.[47]

The negative impacts of climate change on health will be greatest in some of the poorest regions of the world. Many populations are extremely vulnerable to the effects of climate change. This vulnerability is linked to the location of the population (i.e., ecology), to the current infrastructure (i.e., access to sanitation and medical care), to the availability of clean water, to the reliability of food production, and to many other social factors.

If a community is already suffering from malnutrition or outbreaks of bacterial diseases due to lack of sanitation and clean water, an extreme weather event or changes in ecosystem-mediated disease will have devastating results. If climate change facilitates the population growth and range expansion of vectors and pathogens, these vulnerable communities will succumb to increased frequency of disease.

46. At the time of the writing of this chapter, the 2007 G8 summit has just completed, and the governments involved have agreed that some response is needed. The exact response is not yet agreed upon.

47. Robins 1999.

Creation is suffering (Rom 8:19–22), and as a result, many people suffer due to diseases, lack of water, and crop failure. While there may be disagreement about the role that humans play in environmental degradation, it is clear that we are able to change our behavior in such a way as to alleviate suffering for many. We are called to love our neighbors, yet we consume resources at rates that are not sustainable. This has immediate consequences for many neighbors living in the developing world, and long-lasting consequences for our future neighbors.

REFERENCES

Boff, L. 1997. *Cry of the earth, cry of the poor*. Maryknoll, NY: Orbis.

Checchi, F., J. Cox, S. Balkan, A. Tamrat, G. Priotto, K. P. Alberti, D. Zurovac, and J.-P. Guthmann. 2006. Malaria epidemics and interventions, Kenya, Burundi, Southern Sudan, and Ethiopia, 1999–2004. *Emerging Infectious Diseases* 12:1477–85.

Corvalán, C., S. Hales, A. J. McMichael, core writing team. 2005. *Ecosystems and human well-being: Health synthesis*. Millennium Ecosystem Assessment. Geneva: World Health Organization.

Farmer, P. 1999. *Infections and inequalities: The modern plagues*. Berkeley: University of California Press.

———. 2003. *Pathologies of power: Health, human rights, and the new war on the poor*. Berkeley: University of California Press.

Glass, G.E., J. E. Cheek, J. A. Patz, T. M. Shields, T. J. Doyle, D. A. Thoroughman, D. K. Hunt, R. E. Enscore, K. L. Gage, C. Ireland et al. 2000. Using remotely sensed data to identify areas at risk for hantavirus pulmonary syndrome. *Emerging Infectious Diseases* 6:238–47.

IPCC. 2007. *Climate change 2007: Impacts, adaptation, and vulnerability*. Cambridge: Cambridge University Press.

Long R. A., D. C. Rowley, E. Zamora, J. Liu, D. H. Bartlett, and F. Azam. 2005. Antagonistic interactions among marine bacteria impede the proliferation of *Vibrio cholerae*. *Applied and Environmental Microbiology* 71:8531–36.

McMichael, A. J., R. E. Woodruff, S. Hales. 2006. Climate change and human health: Present and future risks. *The Lancet* 367:859–67.

Morgan, O., M. Ahern, and S. Cairncross. 2005. Revisiting the tsunami: Health consequences of flooding. *PloS Medicine* 2:491–93.

Morse, S.S. 1995. Factors in the emergence of infectious diseases. *Emerging Infectious Diseases* 1:7–15.

Oreskes, N. 2004. The scientific consensus on climate change. *Science* 306:1686.

Patz, J. A., P. Daszak, G. M. Tabor, A. A. Aguirre, M. Pearl, J. Epstein, N. Wolfe, A. M. Kilpatrick, J. Foufopoulos, D. Molyneaux, D. J. Bradley, and members of the working group on Land Use Change and Disease Emergence. 2004. Unhealthy landscapes: policy recommendations on land use change and infectious disease emergence. *Environmental Health Perspectives* 112:1092-98.

Patz, J. A., A. K. Githeko, J. P. McCarty, S. Hussein, U. Confalonieri, and N. deWet. 2003. Climate change and infectious diseases, in *Climate change and human health*, ed. A. J. McMichael et al, 103-32. Geneva: World Health Organization.

Robins, N. 1999. Making sustainability bite: Transforming global consumption patterns. Journal of Sustainable Product Design, July 1999:7-16.

Shanks, G. D., S. I. Hay, D. I. Stern, K. Biomndo, R. W. Snow. 2002. Meteorologic influences on Plasmodium falciparum malaria in the highland tea estates of Kericho, Western Kenya. *Emerging Infectious Diseases* 8:1404-8.

Slingenbergh, J., M. Gilbert, K. de Balogh, and W. Wint. 2004. Ecological sources of zoonotic diseases. *Revue Scientifique et Technique* (International Office of Epizootics) 23:467-84.

UNPFA. 2005. State of the World Population. Accessed on June 11, 2007. Online: http://www.unfpa.org/swp/index.html

Wilson, J. 2006. Health and the environment after Hurricane Katrina. *Annals of Internal Medicine* 144:153-56.

Walters, M. J. 2003. *Six modern plagues and how we are causing them*. Washington DC: Island.

WHO. 2004. Using climate to predict outbreaks: A review. Accessed June 11, 2007, Online: http://www.who.int/globalchange/publications/oeho401/en/print.html.

4 • THE ECONOMICS OF GLOBAL WARMING

P. J. Hill

I consider two strong biblical themes of particular relevance to our discussion of global warming. The first is our responsibility, as people created in God's image, to be good stewards of God's creation. This is clear throughout the Scripture and is a responsibility we cannot avoid. In fact, it is one we should accept willingly and joyfully.

Second, we must think seriously about the impact of any policy or human interaction on the well-being of the poor, the marginalized and the oppressed. Of course, there are many other aspects of Christian theology that are relevant for the discussion of environmental concerns, but there is enough content in these two themes to give us substantial guidance in our discussion of the important topic of global warming.

Having said that, I want to argue that moving beyond that point of stewardship and concern for the poor requires numerous prudential judgments. We must have a careful, thoughtful examination of evidence and of trade-offs, a recognition of competing weights on values, and assessments of risks and of the probability of various scenarios playing themselves out.

This means that honest, thoughtful Christians can, because of different prudential judgments, disagree with each other on what stewardship and care for the poor look like in the complex world we live in. I say this to remove any perception that I am presenting the only possible Christian position on global warming. I am laying out what I think is a reasonable and scholarly approach to a very difficult problem, namely, thinking through what the Christian response should be to the possibility of substantial global warming. I recognize that other Christians—operating from the same basic premises of our responsibilities—can come to quite different conclusions.

The title I have been given—"The Economics of Global Warming"—I am taking primarily as a question, what should be the policy response to our present state of knowledge? Because we are dealing with a "global commons" problem where people (and nations) are not held accountable for their actions, it is appropriate to think about a global policy response. This is not a problem that will just take care of itself. We cannot rely on what some would consider the laissez-faire solution "Just leave it alone, the market will solve the problem."[1]

As we attempt to craft at least a partial solution to the global warming problem, I will—as expected—be relying heavily upon the science of economics in my discussion. Economics is all about scarcity—the fact that we face trade-offs. Getting more of one thing means we will have to give up something else.

This idea is very important in the global environmental framework. There are a large number of environmental problems and related issues, so we will have to make some choices, and some of those may be unpleasant choices. We cannot have all we want of everything, and an intelligent (and a Christian) policy response means we must understand the trade-offs involved in making decisions, and must carefully weigh those trade-offs. The fundamental question is, what else could we have done with the resources we commit to solving a particular problem?

We can gain some insight into the difficult choices facing us when we look at the three most significant environmental problems for the poor of the world—especially for those living on less than one dollar per day. They are, in order of importance: 1) indoor air pollution, primarily from burning local fuels; 2) water pollution that leads to microbial diseases; and 3) water pollution that leads to parasitic diseases.

As further evidence of the trade-offs involved, if the Kyoto protocol was fully implemented and obeyed (meaning that if the U.S. and Australia signed on and everyone reached their targets), and if the Protocol stayed in force until 2100, we would gain five years on global warming by that date. In other words, the level of carbon dioxide in the atmosphere projected for 2100 would not be achieved until 2105.[2] The annual cost of the

1. This is actually a caricature of laissez faire, because economists who are of that orientation argue that markets only work well if property rights are well defined and transferable. The basic problem of global warming is one of poorly defined property rights, or of a global commons, where individuals take actions that they are not held accountable for.

2. Lomborg 2007, 11.

Protocol has been estimated at $180 billion. However, UNICEF estimates that for about half of this amount, one could give every person in the Third World access to health, education, clean water, and sanitation.[3]

These facts don't give us clear-cut answers as to what should be done. But they do point out the necessity of making choices about how we want to use resources with respect to environmental problems.[4]

One of the most difficult issues in dealing with global warming is the length of time involved and the rather large range of estimates of temperature change. The impact of anthropogenic global warming is cumulative, and the concern lies with the overall level of carbon dioxide in the atmosphere as a result of years of carbon emissions. Thus policy concerns are usually expressed in terms of the impact in 2050 and 2100.

Think back forty-three years to 1964, or ninety-three years to 1914, and ask, if you were trying to construct policy prescriptions in those years, how accurate would your predictions have been about today's technology, world politics, and economic development? Then look at the range of predictions for temperature change that the latest IPCC report gives us of 1.1 to 6.4 degrees Centigrade,[5] and you can see the difficulties one faces. We have to make estimates of the effects of global warming over a long time horizon, with a large range of possible temperature changes.

All of this doesn't mean we shouldn't be making estimates, especially since some of the worst-case scenarios predict large enough costs from global warming that we can't ignore the problem. The fact that carbon dioxide has at least a two-hundred-year lifespan in the atmosphere means we have to think long term. But we should also be somewhat cautious about making bold predictions about the future with confidence.

If we turn to estimates of the costs and benefits of dealing with global warming, one recent estimate receiving a great deal of attention is the *Stern Review*, a preliminary version of which was issued in the fall of 2006 (although it carries a 2007 date).[6] Stern's estimates of the costs of global warming—a 20 percent drop in global consumption per per-

---

3. Lomborg 2007, 19.

4. Of course one can argue that the two issues are not comparable because different policy mechanisms are required to deal with global warming and localized problems such as water pollution or the burning of fossil fuels. However, on that level, it is clear that the political hurdles to dealing with global warming are much more significant than those that exist for solving indoor air pollution, education, and water pollution problems.

5. IPCC 2007, 13.

6. Stern 2007.

son—are large enough to move global warming to the top of any policy agenda. Stern also estimates that carbon emissions could be stabilized at a cost of approximately one percent of GDP, making reductions in carbon emissions an easy policy choice.

However, since the publication of the *Stern Review*, numerous critiques of his methodology have emerged. One of the strongest has come from William Nordhaus, a Yale University economist who has been one of the leading researchers on global climate change.[7] Nordhaus points out that Stern's large estimates of cost are heavily dependent on the fact that he uses close to a zero discount rate for comparing present and future costs and benefits. Although it seems defensible to treat costs to future generations as equal to costs to present people, using a zero discount rate does not fit with how humans react, nor does it satisfy numerous welfare criteria.[8]

If we truly believed that future dollars will have the same worth as present dollars, we would live at an absolute subsistence level now so that we could enjoy large amounts in the future. For instance, if we could earn a 5-percent rate of return, we would never think of purchasing a three-dollar latte, since in thirty years that three dollars would have grown to $12.96. And, given the fact that we value present and future dollars equally, we would clearly choose $12.96 over $3.00.

Likewise, if we have any concerns for our grandchildren, even at the low rate of return of 3 percent, we should minimize our consumption today because every one hundred dollars we save today means our grandchildren can have $1900.22 in one hundred years. Although most of us do care about future generations, almost no one acts as if zero discounting is a sensible way to organize their personal consumption patterns.

In the same way, if one uses a zero discount rate for calculating the costs and benefits of global warming, the possibility of any future change in climate looms so large in present calculations that it makes sense to accept substantial costs now in order to avoid the enormous costs that are potentially possible. This is because one considers all costs that occur on into infinity as equal to present costs. In the *Stern Review*, "more than half of the estimated damages 'now and forever' occur after the year

---

7. Nordhaus 2007.

8. For a discussion of the ethical implications of the choice of a discount rate see Beckerman and Hepburn 2007.

2800."[9] And using the Review's growth projections, we would be justified in reducing annual per capita consumption from $10,000 today (approximately the present average world level) to $4,400 in to order to prevent people living two centuries from now from reducing their consumption from $130,000 to $129,870 from that point on.[10]

Thus standard economic reasoning gives much lower estimates of the costs of global warming than the *Stern Review* does, and also gives little grounds for engaging in massive immediate measures to reduce carbon emissions.[11]

Another major issue with regard to global warming mitigation policies is the impact on the poor people of the world. Much of the discussion of the impact of global warming focuses on the effects of climate change on residents in less-developed nations, but little attention is given to the possibility that significant restrictions on carbon emissions will substantially slow economic growth in those countries. It is important to also remember that trade-offs do exist. Resources spent to lessen the impact of global warming cannot be used to solve other problems.

It is difficult to assess the relative merits of different proposals to deal with the wide range of problems facing humankind, but one of the most ambitious and scientifically based has been carried out under the title of the Copenhagen Consensus. Bjørn Lomborg, a Danish statistician, assembled eight respected economists from numerous universities and countries. The economists who participated were Jagdish Bhagwati (Columbia University); Robert Fogel (University of Chicago), Bruno Frey (University of Zurich), Justin Yifu Lin (Peking University), Thomas Schelling (University of Maryland), Vernon Smith (George Mason University), and Nancy Stokey (University of Chicago).[12]

The economists were asked the following question: "What would be the best ways of advancing global welfare, and particularly the welfare of developing countries, supposing that an additional $50 billion of resources were at governments' disposal?"[13] The group took up the issues of

---

9. Nordhaus 2007, 25.

10. Nordhaus 2007, 26.

11. It should be noted that Nordhaus's climate change model does not suggest doing nothing at this point. Instead, he suggests a modest carbon tax now that will gradually ramp up over time.

12. At the time of the conference, Fogel, North, and Smith were Nobel laureates; since that time, Schelling has also received the Nobel Prize.

13. Lomborg 2004, 605.

climate change, conflicts, malnutrition and hunger, sanitation and water, communicable diseases, financial instability, education, population migration, and subsidies and trade barriers.

Papers were commissioned which took up thirty policy proposals, and care was given to choose strong advocates for each area of concern. The participants debated these proposals in detail and also considered critical appraisals, written by other experts, of each of the proposals. After consideration of each of the projects, the individuals all ranked the proposals in descending order of desirability.

The final ranking was arrived at by taking the median of individual rankings. The panel also agreed that the ranking produced below represented their consensus view. The rankings were:[14]

VERY GOOD

1. Diseases: Control of HIV/Aids
2. Malnutrition: Providing micro nutrients
3. Subsidies and trade: Trade liberalization
4. Diseases: Control of malaria

GOOD

5. Malnutrition: Development of new agricultural technologies
6. Sanitation and water: Small-scale water technology for livelihoods
7. Sanitation and water: Community-managed water supply and sanitation
8. Sanitation and water: Research on water productivity in food production
9. Government: Lowering the cost of starting a new business

FAIR

10. Migration: Lowering barriers to migration for skilled workers
11. Malnutrition: Improving infant and child nutrition
12. Malnutrition: Reducing the prevalence of low birth weight
13. Diseases: Scaled-up basic health services

BAD

14. Migration: Guest worker programs for the unskilled

14. Lomborg 2004, 606.

15. Climate: Optimal carbon tax
16. Climate: The Kyoto Protocol
17. Climate: Value-at-risk carbon tax.

Although one should not take these rankings as the final word on all policies, it is interesting that the three climate change policies ranked at the very bottom of the projects for human betterment.

When faced with the same question, other groups have reached similar conclusions. The Copenhagen Consensus project brought together eighty young college students, 70 percent from developing countries, with equal gender representation. They were given five days to inquire of experts in all of the areas listed above, and they also ranked malnutrition and communicable diseases at the top of the problems that should be dealt with, and climate change next to last.[15] Finally, in 2006 a group of UN ambassadors spent two days debating the priority list and came to similar conclusions.[16]

These attempts to thoughtfully assess the trade-offs involved in any policy proposals ought to give Christians pause when thinking of climate change measures. It may well be that advocating strong immediate remediation policies will come at the cost of substantially harming the poor and marginalized of the world, either because growth rates of their income would be reduced, or because resources spent on remediation could have been used much more effectively to deal with problems they face.

As an example of the relative costs of dealing with particular problems that may be produced by global warming, Lomborg calculates that a targeted policy of direct action to reduce malaria would prevent 850,000 deaths per year over the next century at a cost of $3 billion annually, while a Kyoto-type policy would cost $180 billion annually and would save only 1,400 lives every year.[17] Indur Goklany has calculated numerous other adaptive responses to potential global warming—responses that have been shown to be much cheaper than attempting to deal directly with the problem.[18]

15. Copenhagen Consensus 2006, 645–48.
16. Copenhagen Consensus 2006. They ranked Kyoto as twenty-third and the other climate change proposals as 37–40 out of forty.
17. Lomborg 2007, 1.
18. Goklany 2007.

Finally, one cannot avoid the political-economy issues inherent in dealing with climate change. The atmosphere is a global commons: In other words, people take actions that have an impact on other people far removed, often in other countries in other parts of the world. And if any remediation policies are to be effective, two of the major population centers of the world must be involved: China and India. In China, two 500-megawatt coal-fired power plants are started up each week, which means the coal-fired generating capacity in China increases each year by an amount equivalent to the entire British electrical system.[19]

Therefore any realistic policy measures must recognize the necessity of monitoring carbon emissions all over the world, and must have an effective means of enforcing agreements. Again, this does not negate the argument for emission controls, but it does mean that one should not be overly optimistic about the ease of imposing either a worldwide cap-and-trade policy, or a worldwide carbon tax.

One can gain some insight into the problems of dealing with large-scale commons by examining ocean fisheries. The worldwide fish catch has been falling for several years because the ocean is an open-access resource, i.e. anyone can enter and fish. As is the case with most open-access resources, the "tragedy of the commons occurs," with resource use far exceeding a sustainable rate.[20]

In this case, the science is clear, and successful methods exist for solving the tragedy of the commons in fisheries. Countries have sovereign control over ocean waters two hundred miles from their shores. Within those limits, several nations—especially Iceland and New Zealand—have put in place a regime of Individual Transferable Quotas (ITQs).[21] These quotas specify the annual total allowable catch from a fishery and also partition that catch out among fishers. The total limit is set by fish biologists, and each individual quota is set as a percentage of the total catch, since the annual allowable catch may change as scientists refine their estimates of the reproductive capacity of a particular fish stock.

Despite the success of ITQs and despite the high degree of confidence in estimates of the cost of fishing on the open seas, nations have not

19. Dirty King Coal 2007.

20. The open-access resource that is overused in global warming is the atmosphere. Individuals and nations face no charge for emitting carbon dioxide into the atmosphere. Thus incentives are not in place for appropriate rates of use.

21. Leal 2000.

been able to agree on effective catch limits outside of their boundaries.[22] If nations have not been able to agree on solving a commons problem so straightforward as fishing on the high seas, it does not bode well for any workable international agreements to control carbon emissions, especially since poor countries would probably be agreeing to substantially reduce their rate of economic growth.

In all of the above, I have argued the following:

1) Because of the long time-horizon and wide range of estimates of the impact of global warming, any policy recommendations will carry a high degree of uncertainty.
2) Reasonable estimates of the costs or benefits of responses to global warming place emission-reduction policies toward the bottom of a list of important problems facing humans.
3) One must recognize the potential for substantial harm to the poor people of the world of many recommendations for dealing with global warming.
4) The political problems of securing effective agreement on global warming policies loom large.

However, I do not want to end on a note of despair, recommending we ignore the possibility that global warming will substantially affect humanity. Therefore I close with several recommendations of policy measures that I think are feasible and make sense in view of the state of the debate over climate change.

First, we need to think more seriously about using more nuclear power, both in the U.S. and in other countries. Many who see global warming as catastrophic and requiring immediate action are also opposed to the use of nuclear power. I believe those who think of global warming as an immediate threat should rethink their opposition to nuclear power. It is the major proven source of energy generation that is not carbon emitting and is close to coal in terms of cost.[23]

---

22. An exception is in whaling. The International Whaling Commission, an organization of whaling and nonwhaling nations, has regulated whaling around the world. However, the agreement is very controversial and looks as if it may soon break apart. See "Sharpening Their Harpoons" 2007.

23. Wind power, solar energy, and biomass fuels may become cost effective as technology advances. Continuing research in these areas holds promise, but for the immediate future increased use of nuclear power is the most likely large-scale replacement for

Power generation is responsible worldwide for approximately one fourth of all greenhouse gases.[24] Presently the U.S. receives 20 percent of its electric generation from nuclear (in France it is 80 percent), but a new nuclear plant has not been created in decades because of high regulatory hurdles and the general perception that nuclear plants are too risky. Using nuclear power has its risks, but they are minimal, especially if one believes that global warming has the potential to be a serious problem.

Second, since deforestation is responsible for 18 percent of global greenhouse gas emissions,[25] the wealthier nations of the world should consider more debt-for-nature swaps, where a portion of the debt of a developing country is forgiven in return for stopping the cutting of rainforests. Such swaps suffer from the problem of political instability in the country receiving the debt forgiveness, but some have been successful. Careful structuring of such contracts offers the real possibility of reducing the rate of deforestation.[26]

Finally, nations should remove subsidies that increase the risk of harm from global warming. After Hurricane Katrina, it was decided that the federal government should be responsible for making the flood-prone city of New Orleans habitable again. It is not clear why taxpayer dollars should be used to encourage people to live in risky situations. Likewise most coastal states are providing "last-resort" flood insurance that is attracting more and more coastal residents since insurance companies are either refusing to insure coastal dwellings or substantially increasing their rates. Again, such subsidies encourage risky behavior that makes some of the potential impacts of global warming more severe.

These measures, along with a commitment to ongoing research on global warming and the improvement of non-carbon-emitting technologies, represent my prudential Christian response to the situation given the present state of our knowledge.[27]

---

electricity generation from coal.

24. "A Special Report on Business and Climate Change" 2007, 4.

25. Ibid.

26. Deacon and Murphy 1997.

27. It is also worth starting discussions on a worldwide low-level carbon tax or a cap-and-trade policy. I favor a tax rather than a cap-and-trade policy, because of the enormous political game playing that would be involved in a cap-and-trade policy. A carbon tax involves large political problems also, but those do not loom as large as the ones that exist under cap-and-trade.

REFERENCES

Beckerman, Wilfred, and Cameron Hepburn. 2007. "Ethics of the Discount Rate in the *Stern Review*." *World Economics* (January–March) 8:1, 187–210.

Copenhagen Consensus. 2006. Accessed June 21, 2007. Online: http://www.copenhagenconsensus.com/Default.aspx?ID=797.

Deacon, Robert T., and Paul Murphy. 1997. "The Structure of an Environmental Transaction: The Debt-For-Nature Swap." *Land Economics* 73:1, 1–24.

"Dirty King Coal." 2007. *The Economist*, June 2.

Goklany, Indur M. 2007. "Adaptive Management of Climate Change Risks." The Fraser Institute.

IPCC. 2007. "Summary for Policymakers." In *Climate Change 2007: The Physical Sciecne Basis. Contributions to Working Group I of the Fourth Assessment Report of the Intergovernmental Panel on Climate Change*, 1–18. Cambridge: Cambridge University Press, 2007.

Leal, Donald R. 2000. "Homesteading the Oceans: The Case for Property Rights in U.S. Fisheries." *PERC Policy Series*, (August), Number 19.

Lomborg Bjørn, ed. 2004. *Global Crises, Global Solutions*. Cambridge: Cambridge University Press.

Lomborg, Bjørn. 2007. Testimony before the Subcommittee on Energy and Air Quality joint hearing with the Subcommittee on Energy and Environment of the Committee on Science and Technology, U.S. Congress, March 21.

Nordhaus, William. 2007. *The Stern Review on Economic Climate Change*. Accessed February 7, 2008. Online: *http://nordhaus.econ.yale.edu/recent_stuff.html*.

"Sharpening Their Harpoons." 2007. *The Economist*, May 26.

"A Special Report on Business and Climate Change." 2007. *The Economist*, June 2.

Stern, N. H. 2007. *The Economics of Climate Change: The Stern Review*. Cambridge: Cambridge University Press.

5 · CLIMATE CHANGE: GLOBAL PROBLEM, GLOBAL SOLUTIONS

Noah J. Toly

INTRODUCTION

Climate change is a global problem requiring a global solution. Its causes and consequences are diffuse and inequitably distributed. Both burden the global response with a challenge to coordinate collective action that operationalizes principles of environmental justice, including intragenerational and intergenerational equity. This chapter examines the global nature of the problem, the global response to the crisis, and briefly evaluates the response in terms of environmental justice.

CLIMATE CHANGE: A GLOBAL PROBLEM

Given its near synonymy with global warming, it almost goes without saying that climate change is a global problem in the most obvious senses with which the word global might be used. Causes and consequences of the crisis transcend boundaries of time and space, spanning generations and nations alike. At the same time, the global nature of the crisis—especially the distribution of responsibility and vulnerability—profoundly affects global responses.

Global Causes

While evidence of contemporary climate change has only recently emerged, the phenomenon is far from novel. Records and reconstructions indicate previous dramatic shifts in global average surface temperature, which were accompanied by changes in regional and local climates.[1] Preindustrial changes have been attributed to various natural

1. Jones, Osborn, and Briffa 2001, 662–67; Mann, Bradley, and Hughes 1998,

causes, including slight shifts in the orbit of the earth, variability in solar irradiance, changes in the reflectivity of the planet, and volcanic activity (Crowley 2000, 270–77). Contemporary phenomena of global warming and climate change, however, are set apart by rapid onset, increased impact upon human populations, and "anthropogenesis"—the human origins of the crisis itself.

Evidence that the earth is warming is overwhelming. The twentieth century and beginning of the twenty-first century saw an increase of 0.74° Celsius in the global average surface temperature of the earth, a measure of increased energy that will likely contribute to highly differentiated deviations from normal weather patterns across the globe.[2] That is, deviations from the norm will vary from slight to dramatic over time and space (IPCC 2007a). Differences in temperature are greater at night, near polar extremes, over land, and in winter.

Differences in climate are considerably more variable: projections suggest that trapping more energy in the atmosphere will likely lead to some places being colder and some warmer, some wetter and some drier. Many suggest that the beginnings of such patterns—and not just increases in global average surface temperature—are already observable.

Yet while the existence of climate change itself is generally incontrovertible, its causes continue to be hotly debated. A very small portion of the scientific community argues that the phenomenon is mostly natural in origin. This ever-shrinking voice disputes the human origins of global warming.

Nevertheless the clear balance of scientific opinion and evidence implicates significant human contributions. Since the emergence of climate change as a field of inquiry in its own right, compelling evidence has been collected to support the notion of anthropogenesis.[3] Models including only natural causes cannot account for observed changes in global average surface temperature. Models including only anthropogenic factors approximate observed temperatures, but are not a perfect match. However, models accounting for natural and social causes match extremely well with observed temperatures and trends.[4]

779–87.

2. IPCC 2007a; Karl and Trenberth 2003, 1719–23.

3. For an interesting and accessible history of climate change science, see Spencer R. Weart, *The Discovery of Global Warming* (Cambridge: Harvard University Press, 2003).

4. IPCC 2007a; Stott and others 2000, 2133–37.

The Intergovernmental Panel on Climate Change (IPCC),[5] an international scientific community dedicated to understanding the origins and implications of global warming, attributes global warming to two chief causes: land-use change and increased greenhouse gas (GHG) emissions from the combustion of fossil fuels, the latter being the most significant cause (IPCC 2007a). Releases of sequestered carbon, alterations in the capacity for carbon sequestration, changes in the reflectivity of the planet, and modifications to the composition of the atmosphere have set the global climate on a path toward serious environmental change.[6] GHG emissions are considered the most pernicious of these causes, and current totals—natural and anthropogenic combined—greatly exceed the earth's limited capacity to absorb and recycle such gases (IPCC 2007a).

Estimates of sequestered gases in drilled ice cores and other sources of data about the atmosphere's past detect the beginnings of increased atmospheric concentrations of GHGs in the latter half of the eighteenth century. As many scholars have noted, this coincides with the beginning of the industrial revolution, commonly associated with the emergence of James Watt's steam engine in 1784. This is not inconsequential to contemporary interpretations and actions regarding climate change. GHGs are long-lived in the atmosphere, with lifetimes of between twelve years and fifty thousand years, and carbon dioxide exerts warming effects for between two hundred fifty and four hundred years. Thus emissions from the turn of the industrial revolution are still warming the earth. Since that time, industrial development has accounted for ever-increasing levels of GHG concentrations.

Given the long industrial experience of the Global North, the warming caused by past emissions in such countries is significant. Considering the historical emissions of the Global North, it is fair to say that a vast majority of responsibility for increasing atmospheric GHG concentrations falls upon such countries. Even rapidly industrializing countries, such as China, have contributed little to the problem relative to those countries that have been burning large quantities of fossil fuels since the late eighteenth and early nineteenth centuries. And while countries such as China, India, and Brazil currently emit significant volumes of GHGs,

5. The IPCC was founded in 1988 as a joint effort of the United Nations Environment Program and the World Meteorological Organization.

6. Hasselman and others. 2003, 1923–25; IPCC 2007a; Karl and Trenberth 2003, 1719–23.

other newly industrialized and nonindustrialized countries contribute little to current emissions and have contributed an infinitesimal fraction of historical emissions. So, while the causes of climate change are global, they are not evenly distributed.

Global Consequences

Just as causes of climate change are global, the consequences are global. And just like the causes, the consequences are not evenly distributed. With a 1.1°–6.4°C projected warming of global average surface temperatures over the next century,[7] anticipated adverse effects of climate change are many.[8] For instance, climate change causes biodiversity loss (IPCC 2007b) and is currently among the primary causes—if not the primary cause—of species extinction.[9] It is a chief driver of what Norman Myers has described as a "biotic holocaust" (Myers 1999, 31–39), as the poleward spread of temperate weather dramatically alters habitat at latitudinal and elevational extremes.

Climate change-induced biodiversity loss also implies lost social values. Not merely aesthetic, these values carry significant implications for the sustenance of life and livelihood for millions of people across the globe. As the lynchpin of ecological integrity, the diversity of ecosystems, species, and genetic resources is of central importance to maintaining ecological systems and processes upon which many people directly depend. For example, the bleaching of coral reefs due to even minor changes in water temperature can have dramatic ill effects upon local communities with significant dependence upon marine resources.

Furthermore, biodiversity loss is not the only potential climate-related threat to social values. Others include sea-level rise, increased storm surge, increased intensity and frequency of hurricanes and typhoons, and

---

7. If emissions were stabilized at year-2000 levels over this period, the IPCC estimates an increase in global average surface temperature of 0.3–0.9°C. Of course, emissions already exceed 2000 levels. Various other IPCC scenarios account for a range of emissions. Even a 2°C warming would be equivalent to the difference between the coldest point of an ice age and the preceding and succeeding warm periods.

8. IPCC 2007a; IPCC 2007b; Karl and Trenberth 2003, 1719–23.

9. Bakkenes and others 2002, 390–407; Beaumont and Hughes 2002, 954–71; Erasmus, Barend F. N. and others 2002, 679–93; Midgley and others 2002, 445–51; Parmesan and Yohe 2003, 37–42; Pounds, Fogden, M. L. P., and Campbell 1999, 611–15; Root and others 2003, 57–60; Thomas and others 2004, 145–48.

increased severity of floods and droughts (IPCC 2007a; IPCC 2007b). Sea level rise threatens to flood more than ten percent of Bangladesh, a country densely populated with 133 million people, over the next 100 years (IPCC 1996).

Climate change-induced human suffering is not necessarily a far-off, twenty-second-century problem. In many parts of the world, the effects of climate change are already resulting in hard realities. For example, residents of Malasiga, Papua New Guinea, and parts of Bangladesh find themselves displaced by rising tides (Goering 2007, 1–25; Osnos 2006). Sea-level rise has also made environmental refugees of the citizens of Tuvalu, a small island state in the South Pacific, who are retreating from their homeland and seeking safe-haven and new citizenship in New Zealand (Allen 2004, 44–52; Reuters News Service 2002). Such islands have joined to form the Alliance of Small Island States (AOSIS),[10] which has become a significant contributor to international climate-policy negotiations. Potential displacement is among the group's motivating concerns.

The present human suffering generated by climate change goes beyond the hardships of displacement. Recent research attributes more than one hundred sixty thousand deaths per year—mostly of poor children in Africa, Asia, and Latin America—to climate change-related causes including, but not limited to, extreme weather and the poleward spread of typically tropical diseases (McMichael and others 2003).[11] A study by the Harvard Medical School's Center for Health and the Global Environment

---

10. AOSIS is a network representing the interests of more than forty-three states and observers, many of which share basic climate-related vulnerabilities even if not significant responsibilities. While AOSIS membership is strongest among small-island developing states, it includes members that are not states, not islands, not small, and not developing.

11. For a contrarian position, see Robert E. Davis and others 2004. "Seasonality of Climate-Human Mortality Relationships in US Cities and Impacts of Climate Change," *Climate Research* 26 (2004), 61–76. This article has received much publicity for its very low estimates of projected marginal mortality increases in U.S. cities due to increased heat. The authors note that marginal increases in mortality during summer heat waves may be offset by marginal decreases in exposure-related mortality during the winter months. However, the authors examined only the effects of increased heat in U.S. cities, where air conditioning is ubiquitous even if not universal. The authors do not attend to the relationship between energy use and climate change. Nor do they address the effects of extreme heat in less-affluent communities, other examples of extreme weather, or other warming-related phenomena, such as sea-level rise.

notes the likely increased prevalence of malaria, Lyme disease, West Nile Virus and asthma, among other diseases and conditions (Center for Health and the Global Environment 2005). These concerns accompany those of increased frequency and intensity of extreme weather such as floods, droughts, and heat waves, to make climate change one of the most (if not the most) significant public-health risks facing the world today.

Many believe that climate change will also lead to increased conflict-related human suffering. In 2003 a Pentagon-commissioned study indicated that displacement caused by climate change may be a significant threat to security in the near future (Schwartz and Randall 2003). The United Nations Security Council recently held meetings regarding climate change, only days after a panel of retired U.S. military generals and admirals released a report on "National Security and the Threat of Climate Change."[12] Such reports suggest significant instability-related security and development linkages for climate change.

Notably the consequences of climate change threaten poor populations and future generations in disproportionate measure to their GHG emissions, demonstrating the uneven geographic and temporal distribution of climate change's pernicious effects.[13] Today's rich populations produce more GHG emissions, while the consequent burden of human suffering is borne by today's poor and by future generations.

While the Global North is least vulnerable and most able to adapt, it will not escape this suffering forever. Some consequences may already be evident. Europe's summer of 2003, for example, was the hottest since the sixteenth century, and more than 19,000 deaths on the continent were attributable at least in part to the oppressive heat (Luterbacher and others 2004, 1499–1503). Summer temperatures exceeded average summer temperatures of the period 1901–1995 by 6.0°C. While no single weather event may be attributed to global warming, this summer heat wave was consistent with the predicted patterns of global climate change. Meanwhile, average temperatures of European winters over the past three decades have been the warmest since instrumented readings became available in 1750. According to the Center for Health and the

12. Military Advisory Board. "National Security and the Threat of Climate Change." CNA Corporation, 2006. Accessed February 12, 2008. Online: http://securityandclimate.cna.org/report/

13. Agarwal and Narain 1991; Agarwal, Narain, and Sharma 2002, 171–99; IPCC 2007a; IPCC 2007b; Qader Mirza 2003, 233–48; Roberts and Parks 2007, 404.

Global Environment at Harvard Medical School, the university's analog heat-wave analysis suggests that an event in the U.S. similar to Europe's 2003 heat wave would likely result in more than 3,000 deaths in New York City alone (2005).

The largest polluters will not entirely escape the uncertainty and harmful effects of climate change. But of special concern is (or should be) the fact that global warming victimizes already-vulnerable populations more quickly and more intensely. And the capacity for adaptation to global warming is unevenly distributed around the globe, which exacerbates the global inequalities in human suffering. Capacity for adaptation is generally a function of wealth and geography (Najam, Saleemul, and Sokona 2003, 221–31).[14]

Qader-Mirza has noted that policy mechanisms designed to increase global investment in capacity building for adaptation currently focus on increasing the capability of developing countries to recover from climate-related disasters rather than on adaptation to potential environmental hazards (2003, 233–48). Critics have suggested that these adaptation-investment regimes do not address the increasing magnitude of economic and social vulnerability due to the debt incurred in such a recovery effort. Such practices also represent a significant departure from the polluter-pays principle in favor of a victim-pays principle. In this regard, a preoccupation with adaptation may only intensify already significant inequities in the distribution of climate change's effects and the human suffering caused by them.

GLOBAL SOLUTIONS

Such a problem as climate change, with global causes and consequences, demands a global solution. Promotion of a climate-stable future demands collective and coordinated action. Apart from coordination, it is doubt-

---

14. Some cite this relationship in support of the political-economic status quo, suggesting that we should give less attention to mitigating climate change and more attention to increasing wealth, or that GHG emissions abatement will destroy wealth-building (and, by extension, adaptation capacity-building) opportunities for the most vulnerable. Here the climate change discourse intersects with political economy, begging the question of the production of vulnerability. If one understands our current political-economic system and energy regime as complicit in the production of vulnerability and marginalization—not to mention climate change itself—one cannot expect business as usual to do anything but perpetuate, if not deepen, the production of vulnerability.

ful that such collective action would start soon enough, would include enough actors and a sufficient percentage of global emissions, or would aim high enough to avoid long-term adverse effects.

The Kyoto Protocol

The highest-profile efforts at such coordination began at the United Nations Conference on Environment and Development (UNCED) in Rio de Janeiro, Brazil, in 1992. Five documents emerged from the "Earth Summit," as UNCED was called. These included Agenda 21, The Rio Declaration on Environment and Development, and a statement of principles guiding the management and conservation of forests, as well as the Convention on Biological Diversity (CBD), and the United Nations Framework Convention on Climate Change (UNFCCC). The CBD and UNFCCC were opened for signature at the Earth Summit, and the UNFCCC has enjoyed almost universal participation.

The highlight of the convention has been the emergence of the Kyoto Protocol—opened for signature in 1997 at the Third Conference of the Parties to the UNFCCC (COP-3) and entered into force in 2005, upon fulfillment of the 55/55 criterion[15]—one of the most ambitious international treaties in history. Kyoto represented a second international effort under the auspices of the norm of universal participation, one operationalized as a "North-first" principle by the Montreal Protocol (Hoffmann 2005; Hoffmann 2007). Adopting a principle of shared but differentiated responsibilities, the Protocol sets emissions targets for thirty-nine industrialized nations during its first budget period, 2008–2012. Other countries are exempt from emissions objectives during this initial accounting but are likely to be assigned targets for a second period and beyond.[16] However, cumulative emissions abatement under the Protocol's targets would constitute a 5.2-percent reduction in emissions among Annex B nations by 2010, a far cry from the IPCC's indication that 60-percent reductions from global 1990 levels would be required in order to stabi-

---

15. 55/55 refers to the ratification of the Protocol by at least 55 percent of signatories to the UNFCCC and the representation of at least 55 percent of global emissions by those signatories.

16. The Protocol's Ad Hoc Working Group (AWG) is currently negotiating the foundations for future budget periods, discussing both timing and emissions target determination.

lize sustainable levels of atmospheric GHG concentrations (IPCC 2001a; IPCC, 2001b).[17]

Faced with the prospect of even minimal emissions reductions, negotiators at the sixth Conference of the Parties (COP-6) in 2000 developed the Protocol's flexibility mechanisms, policy devices designed to limit the necessity of domestic emissions reductions in favor of joint action. Among these flexibility mechanisms is "emissions trading." Often described as "hot air," emissions trading is the mechanism by which countries that have achieved emissions reductions in excess of their targets may sell the difference to countries that would rather not achieve their emissions reductions through domestic action.

Notably the majority of "hot air" would be provided by countries of Eastern Europe and the former Soviet Union, the reductions of which have been achieved because of economic recession. Such retrenchments do not represent socially or environmentally sustainable reductions in emissions intensity, and stand to be erased by economic recovery. This suggests that if emissions trading is a viable flexibility mechanism, then parties to the Protocol should consider limiting its use to cases in which emissions have decreased because of concerted efforts at efficiency, conservation, or substitution of non-carbon-based fuels.

Also among flexibility mechanisms are joint implementation (JI) and the clean development mechanism (CDM). JI represents an energy development or a GHG-sequestration project conducted by one country with emissions targets in another country with targets, in exchange for credits equivalent to the difference between business-as-usual (BAU) and actual emissions. For example, Germany may receive credit for a renewable-energy or reforestation project conducted in France. CDM, on the other hand, represents an exchange between a country with an assigned target and a country without such a target. In this case, for example, Germany might receive credit for a renewable-energy or reforestation project conducted in Mexico.

The Parties have also included carbon sinks such as forests—representing already-existing sequestration capacity—in accounting for domestic emissions, effectively reducing the emissions-reduction require-

---

17. These IPCC estimates targeted atmospheric concentrations of CO_2 at 450ppm, a level now widely considered out of reach. More recent studies by the IPCC and others have analyzed the effects of concentrations of 550ppm, 650ppm, 750ppm and higher, and the emissions reductions necessary to stabilize at even these extreme concentrations.

ments of many Annex I and Annex B nations. As part of the Protocol mechanisms, sinks effectively reduce the assigned targets, as they represent the status quo rather than any difference from 1990 levels. While applicable sink credits are capped, there are no limits to the use of "hot air," JI, or CDM.

These policy tools have been designated as means to achieve economically efficient emissions abatement. Unfortunately the implementation of these mechanisms—apart from caps on their use—will likely lead to emissions increases according to BAU projections rather than to abatement (Byrne and others 2004, 429–52). Indeed, phantom emissions reductions from the application of these flexibility mechanisms, applied to the accounts of Annex B countries, ensure a "successful" protocol despite these likely increases in emissions (Toly 2005, 63–78). Parties may claim to have achieved their target reductions despite significant emissions growth at both national and international levels.

While many of the flexibility mechanisms have been introduced into the protocol under great pressure from the government of the United States (the world's largest polluter), this very same government (along with those of other prominent emitters, such as Australia) has unilaterally opted out of participation in the Protocol and has limited participation in international negotiations for the abatement of GHG emissions.[18] Citing Chinese, Indian, and Brazilian lack of targets in the first budget period (and ignoring historical emissions, per capita emissions, differences between "luxury" and "livelihood" emissions, and the near certainty of targets for such countries in a second budget period), it has chosen instead to pursue a domestic agenda of voluntary emissions intensity reductions based upon a "no-regret" strategy that invokes the dubious rhetoric of uncertain causes and effects in global climate change.

"No-regret" policies for GHG-emissions abatement involve the rectification of market inefficiencies and failures in order to reduce emissions at low or no cost, deriving these benefits from increased market efficiency. Such approaches favor preserving the option values associated with capital that might be invested to mitigate climate change, as opposed to the option values associated with a future intact global ecosystem and economy. This approach rejects any relatively costly options for abate-

---

18. Cabinet-Level Climate Change Working Group 2001; White House 2002a; White House 2002b; Wirth 2002, 648–60; Van Vuuren and others 2002, 293–301.

ment in rhetorical deference to the slight possibility that the effects of climate change may not be as vicious as most scientists are projecting. While the scientific community cannot claim to have achieved the same consensus regarding climate change as exists regarding gravity, for example, the evidence for dramatic changes in climate and some level of human contribution to the problem is more overwhelming now than ever. Yet climate change skeptics are undeterred; they continue to deploy the rhetoric of uncertainty as partial justification for "no-regret" strategies.

Beyond Kyoto

The Kyoto Protocol is the only multilateral climate-governance arena with aspirations to universal participation, but it is not the only arena in which global climate governance is taking place. The Asia Pacific Partnership on Clean Development and Climate (APPCDC), for example, represents a voluntary effort to leverage investment in clean energy and development and to promote trade in cleaner technologies, goods, and services (APPCDC 2007). Asia Pacific Partnership members—Australia, China, India, Japan, South Korea, and the United States—"represent about half the world's economy, population, and energy use, and they produce about 65 percent of the world's coal, 48 percent of the world's steel, 37 percent of the world's aluminum, and 61 percent of the world's cement" (APPCDC 2007). Such partnerships, while not insignificant, do not target the level of emissions reduction specified by the Kyoto Protocol.

Other climate-governance initiatives include efforts at the state and local levels. In the U.S., the Western Governors Association and the Regional Greenhouse Gas Initiative (RGGI) are examples of the former. Cities, which are particularly vulnerable to the projected ill effects of climate change and account for 80 percent of anthropogenic GHG emissions, have also undertaken climate governance projects. Transcending municipal boundaries, a number of initiatives have emerged to take advantage of urban connectivity, stimulating intermunicipal dialogue and leveraging global influence.

These include the United States Conference of Mayors' (USCOM) Climate Protection Agreement (CPA), the International Council on Local Environmental Initiatives' (ICLEI's) Cities for Climate Protection (CCP) program, and the International Solar Cities Initiative (ISCI). The CCP program includes more than 650 municipal governments from over thirty countries and is designed around a program of five milestones: emissions inventory and forecasting, emissions-reduction targeting, development of a local action plan, implementation of policies, and monitoring and verification of outcomes (International Council for Local Environmental Initiatives 2007). With 549 cities in 2001, collective emissions of CCP member municipalities were 8% of the global total (Bulkeley and Betsill 2003, 237). Current member cities account for approximately 15 percent of global anthropogenic GHG emissions. ISCI is a considerably smaller initiative, the membership of which currently includes only nineteen cities. However, though ISCI is smaller, it targets "ambitious emission reduction goals . . . which meet 2050 IPCC-consistent targets" (International Solar Cities Initiative 2005).

Multicentric and multilevel governance platforms are important initiatives that go beyond the Kyoto Protocol. Many of them are ambitious and include actors that are typically excluded from strictly multilateral agreements. Such efforts complement but should not replace the kind of universal participation and international cooperation represented by the Protocol.

INTERPRETING GLOBAL CLIMATE GOVERNANCE

Interpretations of climate governance should be grounded in principles of environmental justice. Environmental injustice is the inequitable distribution of environmental risk, and includes intragenerational aspects (distribution of current risk according to gender, race, class, and the like) and intergenerational aspects (distribution of risk over time). An environmentally just response to climate change would minimize intragenerational and intergenerational disparities in the distribution of climate-related risk.

Of course, both intragenerational and intergenerational equity are concerns of the wider discourse regarding climate change and its abatement. However, equity of either sort is a norm largely absent, in an operational sense, from multilateral climate-governance regimes. Kyoto's nod to intragenerational equity through the principle of common but differentiated responsibility is operationalized through the "North-first" version of universal participation, limiting the number of nation-states with targets during the first budget period. However, both principles remain disconnected from emissions targets that, under the Protocol, are more or less arbitrary reductions from national 1990 levels.

The Protocol's flaws go beyond lack of a sustainable target. In fact, as has been argued above, the Protocol's inclusion of carbon sinks and uncapped flexibility mechanisms makes it possible to achieve the Protocol's goals without reducing emissions from 1990 levels or from BAU projections.

Yet in spite of its flaws, Kyoto is an important arena for the continued development of international cooperation for sustainable development. While universal participation has not meant universal commitment to immediate emissions reductions, it should mean universal participation in the development of a global accord for a climate-stable future. Participation does not require unqualified endorsement but instead a willingness to work with others to achieve a common goal.

This common goal should privilege and operationalize principles of intragenerational and intergenerational equity. Among approaches that do so are per capita methods of emissions target setting. In targeting global emissions that would stabilize atmospheric GHG concentrations at a sustainable level by a certain year (such as 450 ppm of CO_2e by 2050), such an approach divides total emissions by world population to determine an appropriate per capita level. This can then be multiplied by the population of any unit (e.g., nation-state, city) to determine a sustainable and equitable target for that unit (Byrne and others 1998, 335–43).

Per capita targets recognize common access to the "sink" characteristics of the earth's atmosphere, oceans, and soils—three primary loci of the carbon cycle responsible for the storage of greenhouse gases. Coupled with limited use of market-based flexibility mechanisms and universal participation, such approaches do justice to sustainability and equity in the global environment. As our modification of the global climate moves from accidental and incidental intervention to purposed management, we should work toward the operationalization of such ideals in environmental governance.

BIBLIOGRAPHY

Agarwal, Anil and Sunita Narain. Global Warming in an Unequal World: A Case of Environmental Colonialism. New Delhi: Centre of Science and Environment, 1991.

Agarwal, Anil, Sunita Narain, and Anju Sharma. "The Global Commons and Environmental Justice - Climate Change." In Environmental Justice: Discourses in International Political Economy, edited by John Byrne, Leigh Glover, and Cecilia Martinez, 171–99. New Brunswick, NJ: Transaction, 2002.

Allen, Leslie. "Will Tuvalu Disappear Beneath the Sea? Global Warming Threatens to Swamp a Small Island Nation." Smithsonian, August 2004. 44.

Asia-Pacific Partnership on Clean Development and Climate (APPCDC). "Asia Pacific Partnership on Clean Development and Climate." Asia Pacific Partnership on Clean Development and Climate. Accessed February 7, 2008. www.asiapacificpartnership.org

Bakkenes, Michel, J. R. M. Alkemade, F. Ihle, R. Leemans, and J. B. Latour. "Assessing Effects of Forecasted Climate Change on the Diversity and Distribution of European Higher Plants for 2050." Global Change Biology 8 (2002) 390–407.

Beaumont, Linda J., and Lesley Hughes. "Potential Changes in the Distributions of Latitudinally Restricted Australian Butterfly Species in Response to Climate Change." Global Change Biology 8 (2002) 954–71.

Bulkeley, Harriet, and Michele M. Betsill. Cities and Climate Change: Urban Sustainability and Global Environmental Governance. New York: Routledge, 2003.

Byrne, John, Leigh Glover, Vernese Inniss, Jyoti Kulkarni, Yu-Mi Mun, Noah J. Toly, and Young-Doo Wang. "Beyond Kyoto: Reclaiming the Atmospheric Commons." In Climate Change: Policy and Politics, edited by Velma Grover, 429–52. Enfield, NH: Science, 2004.

Byrne, John, Young-Doo Wang, Hoesung Lee, and Jong-dall Kim. "An Equity- and Sustainability-Based Policy Response to Global Climate Change." Energy Policy 26 (1998) 335–43.

Cabinet-Level Climate Change Working Group. Analysis of the Kyoto Protocol. Washington, DC: 2001.

Center for Health and the Global Environment, Harvard Medical School. Climate Change Futures: Health, Ecological, and Economic Dimensions. Center for Health and the Global Environment, Harvard Medical School, 2005.

Crowley, Thomas J. "Causes of Climate Change over the Past 1000 Years." Science 289 (2000) 270–77.

Davis, Robert E., Paul C. Knappenberger, Patrick J. Michaels, and Wendy M. Novicoff. "Seasonality of Climate-Human Mortality Relationships in US Cities and Impacts of Climate Change." Climate Research 26 (2004) 61–76.

Erasmus, Barend F. N., van Jaarsveld, Albert S., S. L. Chown, M. Kshatriya, and K. Wessels. "Vulnerability of South African Animal Taxa to Climate Change." Global Change Biology 8 (2002) 679–93.

Goering, Laurie. "The First Refugees of Global Warming." Chicago Tribune, May 2, 2007, sec. 1.

Hasselman, K., M. Latif, G. Hooss, C. Azar, O. Edenhofer, C. C. Jaeger, O. M. Johannessen, C. Kemfert, M. Welp, and A. Wokaun. "The Challenge of Long-Term Climate Change." Science 302 (2003) 1923–25.

Hoffmann, Matthew J. "My Norm is Better than Your Norm: Contestation and Norm Dynamics: Paper Presented at the Annual Meeting of the International Studies Association 48th Annual Convention." Chicago, February 28–March 3, 2007.

———. Ozone Depletion and Climate Change: Constructing a Global Response. New York: State University of New York Press, 2005.

Intergovernmental Panel on Climate Change (IPCC). "Summary for Policymakers." In Climate Change 2007: The Physical Science Basis. Contribution of Working Group I to the Fourth Assessment Report of the Intergovernmental Panel on Climate Change, edited by S. Solomon, D. Qin, M. Manning, Z. Chen, M. Marquis, K. B. Avery, M. Tignor, and H. L. Miller, 1–18. Cambridge: Cambridge University Press, 2007a.

———. "Summary for Policymakers." In Climate Change 2007: Impacts, Adaptation and Vulnerability. Contribution of Working Group II to the Fourth Assessment Report of the Intergovernmental Panel on Climate Change, 7–22. Cambridge: Cambridge University Press, 2007b.

IPCC, editor. Climate Change 1995: The Science of Climate Change. Cambridge: Cambridge University Press, 1996.

———, editor. Climate Change 2001: Impacts, Adaptation, and Vulnerability. Cambridge: Cambridge University Press, 2001a.

———, editor. Climate Change 2001: The Scientific Basis, edited by J. T. Houghton, Y. Ding, D. J. Gripps, M. Noguer, van der Linden, P. J. and D. Xiaosu. New York, NY: Cambridge University Press, 2001b.

International Council for Local Environmental Initiatives. "ICLEI Global: Climate Protection." Accessed February 7, 2008. Online: http://www.iclei.org/index.php?id=800

International Solar Cities Congress 2006: The ISCI Vision. (2005). The original Web site from the 2006 Oxford conference has been deactivated. Yet the information is available online. Accessed February 12, 2008. Online: http://64.233.167.104/search?q=cache:R4BZoqoaJPIJ:www.energiasrenovables.ciemat.es/adjuntos_agenda/SolarCitiesBrochure.pdf+oxford+international+solar+cities+congress+20 06+vision+mills&hl=en&ct=clnk&cd=1&gl=us&client=firefox-a

Jones, P. D., T. J. Osborn, and K. R. Briffa. "The Evolution of Climate over the Last Millennium." Science 292 (2001) 662–67.

Karl, Thomas R. and Kevin E. Trenberth. "Modern Global Climate Change." Science 302 (2003) 1719–23.

Luterbacher, Jurg, Daniel Dietrich, Elena Xoplaki, Martin Grosjean, and Heinz Warner. "European Seasonal and Annual Temperature Variability, Trends, and Extremes since 1500." Science 303 (2004) 1499–1503.

Mann, Michael E., Raymond S. Bradley, and Malcolm K. Hughes. "Global-Scale Temperature Patterns and Climate Forcing Over the Past Six Centuries." Nature 392, (998) 779–87.

McMichael, A. J. et al., editors. Climate Change and Human Health: Risks and Responses. Geneva: World Health Organization, 2003.

Midgley, Guy F., Lee Hannah, M. C. Rutherford, and L. W. Powrie. "Assessing the Vulnerability of Species to Anthropogenic Climate Change in a Biodiversity Hotspot." Global Ecology and Biogeography 11 (2002) 445–51.

Military Advisory Board. "National Security and the Threat of Climate Change." CNA Corporation, 2006. Accessed February 12, 2008. Online: http://securityandclimate.cna.org/report/

Myers, Norman. "Biotic Holocaust." National Wildlife Federation (March/April 1999) 31–39.

Najam, Adil, Huq Saleemul, and Youba Sokona. "Climate Negotiations Beyond Kyoto: Developing Countries Concerns and Interests." Climate Policy 3 (2003) 221–31.

Osnos, Evan. "The Ocean Is Slowly Claiming Malasiga. They Say It's Global Warming." Chicago Tribune, August 20, 2006, sec. 1.

Parmesan, Camille, and Gary Yohe. "A Globally Coherent Fingerprint of Climate Change Impacts Across Natural Systems." Nature 421 (2003) 37–42.

Pounds, J. Alan, Fogden, M. L. P., and J. H. Campbell. "Biological Response to Climate Change on a Tropical Mountain." Nature 398 (1999) 611–15.

Qader Mirza, M. Monirul. "Climate Change and Extreme Weather Events: Can Developing Countries Adapt?" Climate Policy 3 (2003) 233–48.

Reuters News Service. "Tuvalu Seeks Help in U.S. Global Warming Suit." August 30, 2002.

Roberts, J. Timmons, and Bradley C. Parks. A Climate of Injustice: Global Inequality, North-South Politics, and Climate Policy. Global Environmental Accord. Cambridge, MA: MIT Press, 2007.

Root, Terry L., Jeff T. Price, Kimberly R. Hall, Stephen H. Schneider, Cynthia Rosenzeig, and J. Alan Pounds. "Fingerprints of Global Warming on Wild Animals and Plants." Nature 421 (2003) 57–60.

Schwartz, Peter, and Doug Randall. An Abrupt Climate Change Scenario and Its Implications for United States National Security. Global Business Network, 2003.

Stott, Peter A., S. F. B. Tett, G. S. Jones, M. R. Allen, J. F. B. Mitchell, and M. R. Jenkins. "External Control of 20th Century Temperature By Natural and Anthropogenic Forcings." Science 290 (2000) 2133–37.

Thomas, Chris D., Alison Cameron, Rhys Green, E., Michel Bakkenes, Linda J. Beaumont, Yvonne C. Collingham, Erasmus, Barend F. N. et al. "Extinction Risk from Climate Change." Nature 427 (2004) 145–48.

Toly, Noah J. "Changing the Climate of Christian Internationalism: Global Warming and Human Suffering." The Brandywine Review of Faith and International Affairs 2 (2004) 31–37.

———. "Climate Change and Climate Change Policy as Human Sacrifice: Artifice, Idolatry, and Environment in a Technological Society." Christian Scholar's Review 35 (2005) 63–78.
Van Vuuren, Detlef, Michel den Elzen, Marcel Berk, and Andre de Moor. "An Evaluation of the Level of Ambition and Implications of the Bush Climate Change Initiative." Climate Policy 2 (2002) 293–301.
Weart, Spencer R. The Discovery of Global Warming. New Histories of Science, Technology, and Medicine. Cambridge: Harvard University Press, 2003.
White House. "Executive Summary of the Bush Climate Change Initiative." Accessed February 12, 2008. Online: http://www.whitehouse.gov/news/releases/2002/02/climatechange.html. Washington, DC: 2002a.
———. "President Announces Clear Skies & Global Climate Change Initiatives." Transcript of speech delivered at Silver Spring, MD, at the National Oceanic and Atmospheric Administration (NOAA); transcript released February 14, 2002. Accessed February 12, 2008. Online: http://www.whitehouse.gov/news/releases/2002/02/20020214-5.html. Washington, DC: 2002b.
Wirth, David. "The Sixth Session (Part Two) and Seventh Session of the Conference of the Parties to the Framework Convention on Climate Change." The American Journal of International Law 96 (2002) 648–60.

PART 2

A Christian College Takes Some Initial Steps

6 · BIG SCIENCE, BIG GOD

Sir John T. Houghton

I've addressed my talk this morning "Big Science, Big God." Because there is a common belief that science and religion are opposed to each other and don't mix, the expression "big science, big God" may seem to be an oxymoron. But I've deliberately put science and religion together because I believe they are not in opposition. In fact, the idea that they are opposed is a relatively recent idea. I hope that by thinking more carefully and deeply about them both, I will persuade you that science and religion support each other in ways that are mutually enriching.

My own story as a scientist began over fifty years ago. The most important event in my early scientific life was the launching of the first Sputnik satellite by the Russians in 1957. I guess that predates many of you in this audience! In 1960 the United States launched the first weather satellite. Along with others, I began to think of what could be done to observe the Earth, the atmosphere, the oceans—the whole of the Earth system—from space. We were presented with this remarkable opportunity of doing something quite new in learning about the *global* atmosphere that had not been possible before.

And so it was first satellites and then computers that transformed the science of meteorology, the science of weather forecasting and the science of understanding the climate. And I was privileged to be part of that transformation. During the 1970s, I worked with NASA—your space administration—building instruments to observe the Earth from space on four separate missions, followed by a mission to Venus in 1978.

Venus is a bit closer to the sun than we are, but its surface is a dull red heat. And why is it so hot? Because the atmosphere is almost pure carbon dioxide, and the greenhouse effect on Venus is enormous. This is a very good example of global warming, which I'll talk about in my lecture this evening.

This morning I would like to talk briefly about the universe. Scientists over the last 60 years have been working to bring together the physics of the very small, such as the tiny particles that make up the nuclei of atoms, and the very big, such as the far-off galaxies in outer space. The physics of these have come together in a remarkable way to describe the universe as we know it. The evidence points strongly to a universe that began about 14 billion years ago in what is known as the "Big Bang," when all matter and energy, concentrated in an extremely small volume of unbelievable high density and temperature, began to expand. It has continued expanding ever since.

Let me quickly mention three things about the universe: its size, its energy, and its precision. Imagine the Sun as a golf ball somewhere in the middle of this chapel; the Earth would then be a grain of sand roughly where I am. The nearest star would be a hundred miles away. Space is that empty. With the naked eye and a really clear sky, it is possible to count about three thousand stars. But in the Milky Way—the galaxy of which our Sun is a member—there are one hundred billion stars. In the universe as a whole, there are about a billion galaxies. Multiply these numbers together, and we find the total number of stars in the universe. From the farthest ones, the light takes over 10 billion years to reach us. The universe is mind-bogglingly enormous in both space and time.

The energy in the universe is no less stunning. We are familiar with volcanoes, earthquakes or thunderstorms, but these are minuscule compared with what happens in the rest of the universe. The biggest event of all was the Big Bang at the universe's beginning. As matter expanded from the Big Bang, regions of high density condensed into stars. Stars shine from the release of nuclear energy (released as hydrogen is turned into helium), matter being lost and energy gained. Then nuclear reactions inside stars form other elements: carbon, nitrogen, oxygen, and all the way up the Periodic Table to iron. Big stars, as they become old, explode as supernovae; in these explosions, heavier elements are formed, for instance platinum, lead, gold, and uranium. Then from the debris from these explosions, new stars are formed. Our Sun is such a second-generation star. From the rich material around our Sun—containing all the ninety-two naturally occurring elements—the planets were formed, including our Earth. What energy we find in the universe!

What about precision? We are familiar with the very exact movements of stars and planets in the sky. But the Big Bang doesn't sound like anything very precise. However, science demonstrates its extreme precision. The Big Bang force was driving the universe's expansion with gravity trying to pull it back. These forces had to balance to one part in 10 to the power of 60. That's a one with sixty zeros after it. And if you think that is a big number, just listen for an even bigger one. Considering the entropy (or the way the universe is ordered) raises the question, what sort of order was needed at the beginning of the Big Bang? According to Sir Roger Penrose, a distinguished Oxford mathematics professor who has studied this entropy problem, it had to be set with a precision of one part in 10 to the power of 10 to the power of 123.[1] Now if all the trees on Earth were turned into paper and all that paper filled with zeros, there would be nothing like enough zeros to describe that number. If a zero were placed on every atom in the universe, there still would be nothing like enough zeros to describe that number. What fantastic fine-tuning!

Size, energy, precision—all beyond our wildest imagination. And for humans to exist, the whole universe is needed with its enormous size and timescale, its energy, and its precision. This realization begs the question that many scientists have asked: was the universe designed with humans in mind?

And despite the complexity I have talked about, it's often said that the most complex object in the universe is the human brain. Amazingly, our brains have the capacity to understand something of the universe's design and structure. We find the universe to be ordered according to scientific laws that we can discover—the law of gravity, Newton's laws of motion, the laws of quantum mechanics, and so on. Where do they come from? They are not invented by human brains, but they are discovered. They, too, were part of God's creation. They are God's laws, and the science that humans explore is God's science.

Albert Einstein once said the most incomprehensible thing about the universe is that it is comprehensible. This comes from a unique characteristic we possess; we've been made in God's image—Genesis 1:26—which brings with it capacities of understanding and creativity. Paul, in his epistle to the Romans says that creation leads us to knowledge of God—his "invisible qualities, eternal power and divine nature have been clearly seen, being understood from what has been made" (Romans

---

1. See Roger Penrose, *The Emperor's New Mind: Concerning Computers, Minds, and the Laws of Physics* (Oxford: Oxford University Press, 1989).

1:20)—so that we are without excuse. If that was true in Paul's day, how much more true is it in our day today, with our much greater knowledge of the creation?

So what sort of God are we talking about? Did God just set up the laws, light the blue touch-paper, set it off, and retreat to a safe distance without any further engagement? This God is commonly known as a deist God. Many scientists are willing to accept intelligence behind the universe. Einstein described himself as a deeply religious nonbeliever who believed in a deist God. Even Richard Dawkins acknowledges a god in that sense, although he doesn't want to use the word "god." But in trying to say that science has disproved God, people like Dawkins are going completely outside the boundaries of science and misusing it. Science answers *how* questions, not *why* questions. Science neither proves nor disproves the existence of God. The view that science tells the *whole* story is not only biased, it's completely wrong.

Let me now say something about "intelligent design"—a phrase we often hear these days. It is arguments from scientists like Dawkins, who passionately say that science is disconnected from God, that have stimulated what is known as the Intelligent Design (ID) movement. Its proponents argue that there are areas of science, especially those concerned with the evolution of living systems, where the amount of complexity is such that explanation on the basis of scientific law is impossible. They call them "areas of irreducible complexity" and argue that they must have been intelligently designed by a supernatural agent. Some things therefore belong to science, and some belong to the supernatural.

This approach has big problems. The first and most obvious is that as scientific knowledge grows, so does scientific understanding. Things that seem impossible to understand today may eventually come within the grasp of scientific description. If some things are labeled today as due to direct divine action and sometime later a scientific description emerges, the supposed supernatural action is no longer required. This "God of the gaps" is bound to diminish as science advances.

The second problem with the ID approach is even more fundamental. It's based on a misconception of the nature of scientific law. These laws are not invented by scientists; they are an expression of the creator God's orderly activity. The whole of creation is God's intelligent design—both the parts where we've discovered some of the laws describing their control (they are God's laws!) and the parts where as yet we have no description in terms of scientific law. The arguments of the ID movement are based on a misunderstanding of the nature of science and lead to a God who is far too small. I believe it is vital that Christians—especially Christians who are scientists—take the high ground and insist that the creator God is the Originator and the Sustainer of the whole of creation, and that our scientific descriptions all provide evidence of his intelligent design.

In speaking in this way, I could perhaps be accused of oversimplifying the views of the ID community. There are in fact many detailed points to be discussed. Most of the examples of ID that are put forward are from biology; however, I am not a biologist, so I cannot comment on them in detail. Francis Collins, a distinguished biologist and head of the Genome project, has addressed some of them in his excellent 2006 book *The Language of God*.[2]

Some Christians—when speaking about science—give the impression that they are presenting people with a dilemma: either you believe in science or you believe in God. I believe this is a completely false dilemma, because what science is doing is describing God's creation and the way he has created it. What I therefore want to emphasize most is a basic point that is absolutely fundamental: our science is God's science and belongs to him. It's something I've believed from my early years as a scientist. I've been exploring the relationship between science and faith and the connections between them for most of my life. It is a most rewarding exploration.

Now I would like to mention the Intergovernmental Panel on Climate Change (IPCC), which I was privileged to chair for fourteen years. The panel's purpose was to provide an accurate assessment of the science of climate change—a very complex area of science. Hundreds of scientists—including most of the world's leading climate scientists in the world—came together with different backgrounds, personal agendas and preconceived ideas about what the science should be like. Yet when we really got down together and agreed under the discipline of science to be absolutely honest, the honesty won through. We were able to generate IPCC assessments that have been invaluable in providing reliable information to the world.

---

2. Francis S. Collins, *The Language of God: A Scientist Presents Evidence for Belief* (New York: Free, 2006).

The data on climate change is enormously large and varied. We needed to look at it all. Small parts of the data can be selected to prove almost anything. What is needed is to find the best balance that includes all the evidence. The process of extracting the best balance tends to be a humbling one. Thomas Huxley, a nineteenth-century scientist, talked about being humble before the facts of science that present a picture of the world, the universe, the whole of creation so wonderful, so complex, and yet so orderly. And yet we are able to understand some of it. I often talk about the three *h*'s: honesty, holism and humility. Each is important in our approach to science, and indeed in our approach to many things in our lives.

I would like to add one further thing. When facing the responsibility of chairing some of those large and difficult meetings, I was aware of the prayers of Christian people on my behalf, both within the IPCC group and throughout the world. I can pay tribute to the strength that comes through prayer and through knowing that people are praying.

Let me now return to the deist God I introduced earlier and ask, Is there more to the Creator than a deist God? I still remember how the scientist who was the supervisor for my doctorate program in Oxford years ago used to say, "I can believe in a God who made it all and who made the laws of nature. But a God who is interested in me, I can't believe in that. Absolutely not." But this is too simple of a copout. We may appear minuscule in terms of the size of the whole universe, but God is enormously big—bigger than we can ever imagine. There is no reason to argue that he can't be interested in me. Almost by definition, God is big enough to be interested in every one of us.

Is there any evidence in science that might point towards a personal God? Stephen Hawking is a cosmologist with Lou Gehrig's disease who wrote the bestseller *A Brief History of Time*,[3] which sold ten million copies in hardback. (With my books, if I sell one tenth of one percent of that, I think I'm doing very well!) It's a remarkable book, known as the "most unread bestseller in the world"—it is not an easy read. Hawking talks in this book about the mind of God. He would say he is not a believer. He would say he essentially believes in God in a sort of deist way. But his book plays with the idea of the *mind of God*, but fails to explain what he

---

3. Stephen W. Hawking. *A Brief History of Time: From the Big Bang to Black Holes* (Toronto: Bantam, 1988).

means by God's mind. Is he, perhaps inadvertently, attributing personal qualities to God?

Earlier I outlined evidence that might suggest that the universe has been designed with conscious beings like ourselves in mind. We also possess the capability to understand and appreciate something of the universe's grand design: its order, precision, its mathematical basis, and perhaps most surprising of all, its reliability and consistency. And all this is possible because we have minds, with consciousness and self-awareness.

But what is our consciousness or our self-awareness? Scientists ask these questions—in fact, understanding the science of the mind is perhaps the greatest challenge faced by modern science. But so far science cannot even come up with a good definition of what it means to be conscious. For instance, suppose we are told there is either a computer or a person in a closed room with which or whom we can communicate through a keyboard. How do we decide which it is? No adequate test has yet been formulated. And yet we all know we have consciousness, self-awareness, and freedom of action.

Since we possess these qualities of personality (consciousness, self-awareness, and freedom of action), we can argue that they must also be characteristics of the creator God. After all, we are made in his image. God, the maker of the universe, is not merely a mathematician or a machine. Such a God would be completely inadequate and uninteresting. But a God with personality, to whom we might relate, really grips our attention—although it's an idea that Dawkins in his book *The God Delusion* dismisses out of hand, providing no argument, scientific or otherwise, for its dismissal.[4]

Forming a personal relationship with the One who created the fantastic universe is the most wonderful and exciting possibility open to us as humans. It is something worth pursuing more than anything else in the world. In fact, our scientific exploration—our asking the question "Why?"—has led us to ask whether the creator God might be known by us. As William Temple, archbishop of Canterbury, wrote over sixty years ago, "Natural theology (the study of what you can learn about God from creation) ends with a hunger for that Divine Revelation which it began by excluding from its purview."[5]

---

4. Richard Dawkins, *The God Delusion* (Boston: Houghton Mifflin, 2006).
5. William Temple, *Nature, Man, and God* (London: Macmillan, 1935), 306.

A schoolboy began an essay on science and religion with the sentence: "The difference between science and religion is that science is material and religion is immaterial." That (with its ambiguity of meaning) may seem to express a simple and easy divide, but I believe it is a misconception of both science and religion. The material and the spiritual are not unrelated. Our involvement with the material world, and our scientific study of it, are not outside God's Big Picture but intimately woven into it. The world desperately needs a personal God. Many Christians need a personal God. How personal is your God? Is he nearer to you than hands and feet? Is he somebody you really know? Because if you don't, the possibilities of knowing a personal God are enormous.

Let me take you back three or four hundred years to the birth of modern science as we know it. A group of pioneering scientists that included Isaac Newton, Robert Boyle, Christopher Wren, John Ray, and many others met together regularly in Oxford or London to exchange information about their latest experiments as they excitedly investigated the working of nature in all its aspects. Many of them were Christians and believed their pursuit of science was for the glory of God. They spoke about God's revelation in the form of *two books*: the book of God's works as found in his creation and investigated by science, and the book of God's words as found in the Bible. That God has revealed himself in these two ways is a powerful idea.

In fact, the idea is much older. In particular it is embedded in Psalm 19, a psalm I encourage you to read. It begins by declaring: "The heavens declare the glory of God." Its first six verses speak of God's works in creation, the next three about God's words in Scripture. The final verses enthuse about the value of God's Word, and encourage us to apply the Word to our actions, words and thoughts. David, who wrote the psalm, could only see about three thousand stars, and only had a fragment of God's Word in the books of Moses. Yet he enthused about both God's works and words.

We know so much more of God's works and God's Word. Most importantly, we have the person of Jesus: the perfect image of God; the Son of Man and the Son of God who himself became part of creation. And God couldn't have given us a stronger message about his commitment to creation than the person of Jesus. But we live in a world where God is ignored and the Bible is largely unknown. God's rules are not followed, and people do their own thing, think what they want, and do what they like. That's the modern way. When the world is seen in this subjective way, facts are ignored. Even the objective truth in science is questioned and viewed as just another opinion.

Science and theology together show something very important. Both are talking about objective truth: objective truth about the universe, objective truth about ourselves, objective truth about God. This has big implications for our care for creation—a subject that I'll be talking about tonight.

Finally, let me introduce you to a passage in the book of Proverbs—Proverbs 8:22–31—where we have a beautiful expression of the wisdom of God in the works of creation. Wisdom is personified in this passage as God's "craftsman at his side," "filled with delight day after day, rejoicing always in his presence, rejoicing in his whole world, and delighting in mankind" (vv. 30–31, NIV). Because we also are creative, we can also—in some small way—share in the sheer delight experienced by God the Creator. In the New Testament, this personified wisdom is identified with Jesus (1 Corinthians 1:24). In the early verses of John's gospel, Jesus is described as the agent of creation "through whom all things were made." Paul describes Jesus as the Creator and the Sustainer of the universe: the one "by whom all things were created" and "in whom all things hold together" (Colossians 1:15–17). It is in Jesus, the Word made flesh (John 1:14), that the spiritual and material come together. The whole of creation is involved: "God so loved the cosmos . . ." (John 3:16). It is Jesus who, as the Originator and Redeemer of the whole creation, is at the center of God's Big Picture. He continues at the center as we anticipate new heavens and a new earth—a transformed heaven and a transformed earth—to which Jesus's resurrection into a transformed body points us.

One of the most important hymnbooks of early Methodism was the *Olney Hymns*, published first in 1779. It was here that John Newton's hymn "Amazing Grace" was first published. Another fine hymn in that collection, though much less well known, is one by the poet William Cowper. It is based on the passage from Proverbs to which I've just referred. It beautifully describes the wisdom of God in creation and in Jesus. Here it is:[6]

---

6. William Cowper, "Ere God Had Built the Mountains," in *The Olney Hymns: In Three Books*, compiled by John Newton, 1779.

Ere God had built the mountains,
Or raised the fruitful hills;
Before he filled the fountains
That feed the running rills;
In me, from everlasting,
The wonderful I AM,
Found pleasures never wasting,
And Wisdom is my name.

When, like a tent to dwell in,
He spread the skies abroad;
And swathed about the swelling
Of ocean's mighty flood;
He wrought by weight and measure,
And I was with him then;
Myself the Father's pleasure,
And mine, the sons of men.

Thus wisdom's words discover
Thy glory and thy grace,
Thou everlasting lover
Of our unworthy race!
Thy gracious eye surveyed us
Ere stars were seen above.
In wisdom thou hast made us,
And died for us in love.

And couldst thou be delighted
With creatures such as we!
Who when we saw thee, slighted
And nailed thee to a tree?
Unfathomable wonder,
And mystery divine!
The voice that speaks in thunder,
Says, Sinner I am thine!

7 · THE GREENING OF WHEATON COLLEGE: AN UNLIKELY TREE HUGGER

Ben Lowe

How do you become a tree hugger?

First we need to figure out what makes someone a tree hugger. I once raised this question in a Sunday school class of about fifty junior- and senior-high kids. I was teaching that day and started by playing the word-association game. This is a fun activity where someone throws out a random word and everyone yells out the first thought that comes to mind when they hear it.

If you ever play this game and want a strong reaction, I recommend trying the word "tree hugger." A barrage of outspoken ideas flew right back at me: "liberals," "vegetarians," "drugs," "organic," "smelly," "drugs," "hemp," "drugs," "hippies," "drugs." I could go on, but I think you get the idea.

So if you want to become a tree hugger, then, based on this feedback, it seems you should hop the next train out to Oregon, join a commune in the woods, wear clothes made out of hemp, and smoke pot. Does that sound about right? This almost goes without saying, but you should probably avoid enrolling at a leading Christian liberal-arts college (like Wheaton) where you attend three chapels a week, refrain from drinking any alcohol, and only dance on campus at a few college-sponsored events per semester.

That is what I did—the latter, not the former. I really wanted to attend Wheaton College, so I took a year off from high school, worked full-time at Chick-fil-A, and saved enough money to enroll in the fall of 2003. I was certainly not on track to become anything close to a tree hugger, and if you look over my life story, I am probably one of the most unlikely people to qualify for such a label.

I was born and raised in Singapore—the only 100-percent urbanized nation in the world—where my parents were missionaries with the

Overseas Missionary Fellowship. Singapore is a tiny island off the tip of the Malaysian peninsula in Southeast Asia, but don't let its size fool you. This little country packs a significant economic punch and is home to four and a half million people, all crammed into just under three hundred square miles of developed landscape. As one of the busiest sea- and airports in the world, Singapore is really just one big, modernized city—about as far away from true wilderness as you can get.

National pride is very important to Singaporeans, so they maintain everything meticulously. It is rumored that the city is so clean, you can even eat off the street. (However, I probably wouldn't test this hypothesis.) In a clean city like Singapore, it is not surprising that I remember my school's annual cross-country meets where all the students competed by running (mostly walking, really) three miles through a strip of forest around a water-catchment reservoir. This might seem outdoorsy, but it didn't really count. The trails we ran on were wide and flat, and the sound of traffic always remained in the background. To further ensure our safety, workers were paid to sweep the path clear of scattered leaves before we ran by. Only in Singapore . . .

However, thanks to the government's impressive tree-planting campaign, Singapore is also known as the "Green City." Even so, it's hard to disguise the fact that you're surrounded by a sea of asphalt, high-rise buildings, concrete-lined rivers, and the constant drone of development. I grew up eating like a Singaporean: using public transportation, living in high-rise flats, attending the public schools, and sweating without air-conditioning in the year-round tropical heat. Since I lived in a country that is really one big city, I heard little talk about nature and even less talk about caring for it.

I was raised in a conservative evangelical Christian family and still hold tightly onto the values my parents (and "Focus on the Family" programs) taught me. We had family Bible readings throughout much of my childhood, and my dad often preached at the church we attended. Dad has a PhD in New Testament theology, and Mom has an MA in Christian education. Our dinner conversation typically centered on the dense theological book projects Dad was currently immersed in, which mostly dealt with Pauline theology.

Sure, I've always loved being in nature (though less so when the mosquitoes are out), but this isn't unusual even for someone who grew up in a city. Most of us are awed by images of peaceful sunsets on a lake, majestic snow-capped mountain ranges, and long, sandy beaches dotted with coconut trees. Such picturesque landscapes are often used as backgrounds on computers and in the PowerPoint slideshow during worship services. Many churches still sing hymns like "This is My Father's World," "I Sing the Almighty Power of God," and "For the Beauty of the Earth."

I probably did grow up enjoying day hikes and camping trips more than the average Singaporean, but certainly nothing that would qualify as extreme. After all, I'm the toddler who wouldn't fall asleep unless lulled by the sound of passing traffic. That's right; my parents had to walk me alongside a busy highway every night, or I would lie in my crib wide-awake.

Eighteen years later when it was time to go to college, I knew what I wanted to do. I wanted to attend the best Christian school I knew—Wheaton College—and study to become a pastor. I was on fire for Christ and wanted my life to have the greatest possible positive impact on the world. Becoming a medical missionary was an equally honorable option, but I interned in a hospital and quickly learned that I wasn't called to be a doctor. It was settled then—I would have to become a pastor. It's not that any other vocation was necessarily a bad choice; they just didn't seem to be the best way to serve Christ. And that is all I was interested in doing.

There was only one problem: my parents. They were not keen for me to attend Wheaton, and they didn't want me to major in Bible, theology, or Christian education. Instead they wanted me to attend the most prestigious secular school I could get into and study something in the sciences so I could get a well-paying job when I graduated.

Right. This frustrated me. After all, both of my parents majored in theology during college and have been in fulltime ministry ever since. It seemed somewhat strange that they would have discouraged me from doing the same. But they had good reasons to think this way. All our lives we had struggled to get by, and my parents wanted me to avoid the same uncertainty and financial stress that they had come to expect in ministry.

I could see where they were coming from, but I was still unwilling to give up my dream. So we compromised. I ended up going to Wheaton after all, but I decided to honor their wishes and major in science. It was not the precise field they wanted—which was biomedical engineering—but instead in the most applied field I could find: I became an environmental-studies major.

My plan was to give science a fair try for the first year, at which point I would realize that it really wasn't for me and eagerly switch into theology. Wheaton was renowned for its Bible/theology department, and I was eager to take classes from its professors. After all, I knew that serving Christ meant serving people. I loved nature and the outdoors, but I could not justify wasting time on the environment. People were more important, and their problems far more urgent than saving the whales would ever be. But then two things happened during my freshman year to change what I thought.

First, I learned that the highest calling in life was not simply to study the Bible and become a pastor or missionary. Instead Christ calls us to come alongside him in a much bigger plan—a plan in which good stewardship and caring for his creation play a crucial role. Over the last hundred years, however, evangelicals have developed significant blindspots and have tended to follow a more truncated calling.

As I grew up a missionary kid, one of the most meaningful Bible verses throughout my life has been the Great Commission in Matthew 28:18-20. Before Wheaton, I read it as a mandate to go and evangelize the masses. As such, I focused on memorizing tracts and studying the *Evangelism Explosion* textbook. My goal was to bring as many people as possible to ask Jesus into their hearts. Everything else was secondary.

But through my professors, peers, and classes at Wheaton, I came to read Matthew 28:18-20 in a new and fuller light. Jesus calls us to go and make disciples; I often seemed content just making converts. Christ calls us to obey and teach *everything* he has commanded; I often seemed content obeying and teaching *selections* from what he has commanded. It was not that my vision was wrong; it was just too narrow. God's mission is far greater than I had imagined.

This was true of me, and I think it has been true of the American evangelical church at large. We have done a great job focusing on issues such as abortion and sexual morality. But we have by and large neglected a whole host of commandments to care for the poor, the oppressed, and the creation.

These commandments were not neglected at Wheaton. I learned much about the theology and ethics of creation care from professors like Fred Van Dyke, Kristen Page, Nadine Rorem, Alvaro Nieves, Jim Clark, Jeff Greenberg, David Cook, P. J. Hill, and many others. In fact, my introduction to this topic came when I visited the Wheaton Chinese

Alliance Church during my first Sunday as a freshman. They did not have an English-speaking pastor at that time, so Vince Bacote, a theology professor I would later have for class, was the guest preacher that week. His sermon presented why Christians should care for creation, based on the first two chapters of Genesis.

What a strange coincidence that the first sermon I heard while attending Wheaton was also the first time I ever heard that Christians should care about creation. It is also notable that I was nineteen years old before I first heard a sermon on creation care. Granted, I don't remember much about church from the early years of my life, but the teenage years seem far too long to go without learning an integral component of Christian doctrine and living.

I'll spare you most of the details here, but suffice it to say that my eyes were opened to a fuller understanding of Christ's work and his calling on my life. Creation care is just one of the many issues we care about at Wheaton College, but it was this one issue that really struck home with me.

I came to see that Christ not only created all things but also deeply values and sustains his creation. He has entrusted this good creation to the care of human society and calls us to be faithful image bearers and partners in his work to reconcile all things back to himself and his shalom. The environment was no longer simply something I enjoyed on the side. As a follower of Christ, I shared responsibility for stewarding all creation, both human and nonhuman. And, one day, I would be accountable to the maker to whom all things belong.

If the first lesson I learned was that creation care is an important Christian concern, then the second lesson was that the health of our human race is closely tied to the health of our planet. We do not choose between caring for people *or* the environment—this is a false dichotomy. We are called to care for people *and* the environment.

We all consume resources and impact the environment. In turn, the environment has an impact on us all. It is an unavoidable cost of being alive. Think of flicking on a light switch, turning on the tap, or filling up at the pump. Where does that electricity, treated water, and refined gasoline come from? What impacts occur when we extract, process, and transport all these resources to our homes?

These are resources I used to take for granted, and questions that I rarely thought to ask. But they are such very important and moral questions. If I knew that most of my electricity came from burning coal, then would I not be more careful about leaving the lights on, the computer running, or the fridge door open? We obtain large quantities of coal by blowing up mountains in the Appalachians, resulting in irresponsible pollution and bad health for hundreds of poor communities lacking lobbying power. Not to mention that entire mountains are being destroyed for short-term energy gain. Coal-burning power plants are also currently the largest emitter of mercury, and highly correlated with a greater prevalence of asthma attacks in surrounding regions.

This is only one example of the many cases of environmental injustice happening to our neighbors right here in the United States. As Christians called to love each other, we are right to be outraged at the exploitation happening under our very noses. At the same time, I am sobered and repentant for how my often-careless patterns of consumption have helped drive up the demand for such unsustainable resource extraction.

It is almost a misnomer to label problems such as mountaintop removal as "environmental issues," because of their effects and ramifications on so many other areas of life. Many "environmental" issues can just as accurately be seen as justice issues and human issues. Far from turning our attention away from people in order to work in the environment, we are actually addressing some of their most urgent and relevant needs by working in this broad field. My geology professor, Dr. Jeff Greenberg, often reminds me, "When the land isn't healthy, the people aren't healthy."

Famines, clean-water shortages, overfishing, disease epidemics, depleted energy resources, natural disasters: a lot of the major problems in this world are environmental problems. Over one billion of our neighbors do not have access to safe or adequate drinking water. Every fourteen seconds a child dies from a preventable waterborne disease, making bad water the greatest cause of childhood death worldwide.

Am I—are we, as Christians—prepared to respond to such needs? This might all be old news to you, but when I first heard it, my outlook and priorities changed. I realized that when God calls us to care for people, he's also calling us to care for the environment.

What I was learning during my years at Wheaton began to change the course of my life. As you probably guessed, I remained an environmental-studies major. I now understood that there were many ways to serve God in life, and many fields outside of theology and medicine that desperately needed another Christian witness. The beauty about studying at Wheaton was that I could major in a field like environmental studies, geology, or biology and still take classes in the theology department as well: the best of both worlds, if you ask me.

I also became involved in the startup of our campus environmental club, A Rocha Wheaton. A Rocha Wheaton is the first student chapter of A Rocha, an international organization of Christians in conservation. *A Rocha*—which is Portuguese for "the rock"—began as a field center on a threatened estuary in Portugal. Today it is a member of the World Conservation Union (IUCN), having grown into a diverse community working on projects in Europe, the Middle East, Africa, Asia, and North and South America. Since joining A Rocha, I have been encouraged by the work its members are doing on the frontlines of conservation science, education, and practice in many overlooked places around the world.

At Wheaton our student chapter worked hard and experienced its share of both struggles and triumphs. Great progress has been made, however, and being part of A Rocha Wheaton gave me invaluable opportunities to take what I was learning in the classroom and apply it to actual problems in the real world. The A Rocha network is a great big family, and the community that developed within our own chapter and between members all over the world blessed me with role models, mentors, and inspiration that continue even past graduation.

During my junior and senior years at Wheaton, my involvement in creation-care issues started to build an unexpected reputation among those that knew me. A lot of friends started calling me a "tree hugger." They were joking of course—or at least I think they were. Either way, most of these friends have since started recycling their trash, taking shorter showers, changing to energy-efficient light bulbs and encouraging others to do the same.

Still, it is amusing to think that someone like me would be nicknamed a "tree hugger." I comb my hair, wear normal clothes, worked hard in my classes, never received chapel probation, served as a leader in campus and church ministries—and the list goes on. In many ways, I believe I fit the model of a good, overcommitted Wheaton student. So, how then did I become a tree hugger?

As I stated in the beginning of the chapter, first we must figure out what makes someone a tree hugger. The label clearly has boatloads of negative connotations attached to it. Many have some basis in reality, but none describe in essence what makes someone a tree hugger.

So perhaps it is time to move past the stereotypes and establish a more redeemed definition. Here are four characteristics that I propose as a starting point: A tree hugger is

1) Someone who cares about the environment and its well-being;
2) Someone who cares about human life and its dependency on the environment for survival;
3) Someone who carefully ensures that one's personal impact on the planet and on one's neighbor is sustainable;
4) Someone who takes care to protect one's neighbors and the environment from exploitation and injustice.

Based on this revised definition, I don't think that all tree huggers are necessarily Christians. But I would propose that all Christians are called by God to be tree huggers. It happened to someone as unlikely as me. It can probably happen to you.

Of course this doesn't mean that all of us are called to major in environmental science and devote our lives to devising new clean-energy sources that will reduce global warming. We do need more Christians to choose environmental studies as a vocation, but for everyone to come on board would be quite a bad idea. There are many other important vocations that Christians should pursue. After all, the church is a body, and we wouldn't want it to have all eyes or all left arms.

What I think this framework does mean, however, is that we are all called to do our part to care for creation; to love God, love our neighbor, and be good stewards of the resources that he has blessed us with. To this end, may we all become known as good "tree huggers." And when the world looks on in surprise, it will see that we are no ordinary tree huggers; we hug trees for Jesus.

8 • THE GREENING OF WHEATON COLLEGE: A BIGGER VISION

Ben Lowe

A BIG YEAR

My senior year was a significant one for Wheaton College, which weathered a public-health crisis and an environmental disaster—all in the first semester.

The year began with a mumps outbreak that made national headlines; but I was grateful that the outbreak ended up affecting only about 3 percent of the community. Still, the mumps held on strong for the entire fall semester, resulting in an overworked health center, hand-sanitizer dispensers at Anderson Commons (our cafeteria), and housing relocations to make space available for quarantining suspected cases.

If this had been our big event for the fall, it would have been a sufficiently memorable semester. We were not getting off that easily though.

The real housing headache came on the fateful night of October 3rd, when freak storms dumped record-breaking rain (over five inches in a single hour) on the community of Wheaton. I stood at the entrance to the Macmanis-Evans Hall (Mac-Evans) dormitory and watched sheets of horizontal rain, and bolts of lightening, pound the campus, snap trees in half, and snuff out the power. Unable to soak up all the rain in time, the ground quickly became saturated.

Then it happened. Flash flooding broke out, as rivers of water with nowhere to go turned the Quad into a lake and the Billy Graham Center parking lot into a swimming pool. The floodwaters continued to rise, rushing into the lower Beamer Center and bursting through windows in the Mac-Evans basement. By storm's end, the campus had sustained more than a million dollars in damage, and the guys from an entire basement floor in Mac-Evans were displaced to floor lounges and to other open beds around campus.

By the end of the fall semester, the mumps had lost its hold on campus, and the "flood refugees" started moving back into their repaired rooms. The campus had successfully endured its two "plagues." And as with many challenges or ordeals, a lot of good resulted too.

What stood out most to me is the way the campus community came together during this period. In many ways, the mumps and flood were great community-building events. We united in prayer over the campus and for our friends who were affected. We worked together to help meet the needs that arose. Roommates delivered food, and classmates took notes for those quarantined. Many residents of Mac-Evans opened their rooms and helped lower-level guys move their waterlogged belongings off the floor.

The fine ladies of Williston Hall—the sister dorm to the Mac-Evans lower level—made the rest of us jealous by baking loads of treats for their brother floor. Well, I was never too jealous; the resident assistant for the Mac-Evans lower level ended up staying in my room, so I got to mooch off all the goodies that the Williston folks brought them. As the sign on my door read, ours was "a room for baked goods to fly to." Throughout the semester, I was encouraged to see our Wheaton community rise to meet these challenges and become stronger because of them.

Things started settling down on campus, but the question remained, what would come next? Would we get a new plague with frogs or locusts? Little did we know that the Chicago area would soon be overrun by a naturally recurring cycle of mass cicada hatchings ominously known as "Brood XIII," boasting 1.5 million of the loud insects per acre for miles.

Thankfully the cicada outbreak didn't happen until later in the summer. In the meantime, another completely different community-building event was in the works—the Wheaton Summit.

AN EMERGING VISION

In no way catastrophic but still no less significant than the mumps and the flood, the Wheaton Summit was a groundbreaking gathering of student-leaders in creation care from all over the United States. It began with a small idea: to invite students from nearby colleges to hear Sir John Houghton speak at Wheaton.

At this point, we did not have a very significant or profound vision. Sir John, a world-renowned climate scientist and an outspoken evangelical, was going to come talk about what our Christian response to the global warming issue should look like. Global warming is one of the hottest issues of the day (no pun intended). It is also a serious moral issue that Christians are finally starting to grapple with. Sir John has been dealing with global warming for as long as almost anyone, both as a Christian and as a scientist. Aside from being a professor of atmospheric physics at the University of Oxford and chief executive of the United Kingdom Meteorological Office for many years, he was also the chair of the scientific working group in the Intergovernmental Panel on Climate Change (IPCC) for over a decade.

Given all his credentials and experience, we figured that Sir John would be a speaker worth coming out to hear. However, like popcorn in a microwave, this once-small idea quickly expanded into a bigger vision.

I had been working in the creation-care effort on Wheaton's campus for three years by this time. To be honest, it was often hard, discouraging, and isolating. I was part of the campus environmental club, A Rocha Wheaton, and we were a small group struggling to make progress. The culture on campus was mostly unsupportive of environmental initiatives (issues viewed as too liberal, too controversial, or just not important), and we struggled to make progress and to build interest.

This had recently begun to change through talks in chapel, the support of President Duane Litfin, and the formation of a campus environmental-stewardship advisory committee. As our creation-care efforts started to pick up momentum, we also heard encouraging reports of good sustainability initiatives at other Christian colleges such as Judson and Calvin.

This started us thinking, if we were struggling to make progress on our own, then probably similar small groups on other Christian campuses were facing the same issues. Now that we were finally getting somewhere, though, connecting with each other to learn, brainstorm and fellowship together would really help our project.

The vision for the meeting became one of bringing peers and colleagues in the creation-care effort together for the first time at Wheaton to develop relationships and build much-needed community. In other words, we could develop a creation-care community. It was something I had been longing to see happen for quite some time. So the idea developed to hold a creation-care summit coinciding with Sir John's visit. It would be a multiple-day conference with travel funding to bring fifty student-leaders from across the country to meet with each other and hear from Sir John.

THE WHEATON SUMMIT

Since A Rocha Wheaton had recently been much more active on campus, we took the lead in organizing this summit. We put together a planning team of ten students (including me) and quickly got cracking in the two months we had left before Sir John's visit, three weeks of which fell over Christmas break. In that very short time, we needed to raise over fifteen thousand dollars, plan and set up a three-day conference, invite participants, and line up speakers.

Sound unlikely? I thought so too, but we had a great team working to pull this off—honestly the best team I have ever worked with. The Wheaton Summit planning team included students Lisa Riihimaki (Psychology and Business), Abby Hart (Environmental Studies), Reed Fagan (Environmental Studies), Lisa Jutsum (Political Science), Brittney Dunn (Environmental Studies), Glenn Sharman (Geology), Brendan Payne (History), Jennifer Luedtke (Environmental Studies), and Aaron Wilcoxson (Business/Economics). We spent many late nights together in the home of Wheaton staff member and much-loved mentor Vince Morris, hashing out details and consuming large quantities of homemade fudge and other goodies that his wonderful wife, Ellen, whipped up. I know; it's a tough life sometimes!

Organizing the summit was a tremendous amount of work, but it was worth it. In late January, around eighty representatives from fifteen colleges and from another fifteen organizations converged on Wheaton's campus. Students and faculty came from Gordon College, Eastern University, Dordt College, John Brown University, Messiah College, Azusa Pacific University, and Trinity Western University in Canada among other places. Staff and leaders participating in these sessions represented groups such as the Evangelical Environmental Network; A Rocha: Christians in Conservation; the National Wildlife Federation; and the United Nations Foundation.

Even a couple film crews came and covered what was going on. One team did a documentary on how different faiths are addressing the environmental crises we are facing today. The other group came from A Rocha International (the parent organization of A Rocha Wheaton) to help us record different sessions and to put together a short film. This A Rocha team originally came from the country of my birth, Singapore.

In Singapore we have a very popular tropical fruit called the durian. It's the same size as a small watermelon but has a thick green shell with spikes. It is known in Southeast Asia as the "king of fruit," but it also gives off a strong smell that many foreigners find disgusting. I find it mouthwatering.

When I discovered the Singapore team was coming to the summit, I rushed out excitedly to buy an imported frozen durian to celebrate their arrival. We gathered that evening in the storage room on my dorm floor (to keep the mess and smell down) and cracked open the durian together. We were having a great time until Public Safety officers came to investigate what smelled like a natural gas leak in the building. Apparently the durian smells like natural gas, and the smell had traveled all the way to the fourth floor, where concerned guys put in an emergency call. Oops!

The guys on my floor did not let me forget the "stinking-fruit" incident for quite some time. The rest of the summit went by smoothly, thanks to the hard work of our planning team, and Public Safety did not receive another call on our account.

Those three days passed in a whirlwind of people, events, ideas, and discussions. There were so many friends to make, and so much to talk about with one another, that the summit could have lasted a full week and still would not have been long enough. We heard from many senior leaders in the creation-care movement, including Fred Van Dyke, director of environmental studies at Wheaton College; Matthew Sleeth, executive director of A Rocha USA; Susan Emmerich, CEO of Emmerich Environmental Consulting; Jim Ball, executive director of the Evangelical Environmental Network; Paul Corts, president of the Council for Christian Colleges and Universities; and our own President Litfin. We laid a strong foundation in the biblical creation-care message and also got to know our leaders better. Did you know, for example, that Dr. Paul Corts and his wife drive a hybrid and still take public transportation to work whenever possible? Three cheers for that!

Sir John spoke in several venues at Wheaton, including in chapel, and engaged students with his scientific expertise and ardent Christian faith. Armerding lecture hall was packed out, with students sitting in the aisles to hear him share from his experience chairing the IPCC scientific working group for over ten years.

Sir John was frank and acknowledged that global climate change is an immense problem only expected to get worse. At the same time, he shared a hopeful vision that we can still make a difference if we are more willing to practice the Christian values of sacrifice and sharing. An inspiring example of such positive change came from the Eastern University cohort, who reported that Eastern has successfully switched to 100-percent clean wind energy on the main campus.

COMMUNITY IS KEY

We were intentional about building community during the summit. More than simply attending the sessions, we worshiped, prayed, and broke bread together. Eating together was easy; Wheaton has one of the best college food services in the country, so everyone wanted to feast at the cafeteria. We prayed together every day as well, and took an extended time on the second evening to reflect on what we were learning and to dedicate to God the work ahead.

And at a school like Wheaton, you don't have to go far to find a worship team. Every day began and ended with singing, and we were blessed by two teams who volunteered to lead us. The first team comprised three friends at Wheaton who were not directly involved in the planning but graciously gave of their time and energy to support our efforts. The second featured college students and youth from the nearby Wheaton Chinese Alliance Church, where A Rocha Wheaton had earlier held a creation-care Sunday school series.

There is no magic bullet or secret recipe here. We simply invested time and effort into developing relationships and connecting with each other. In the end, we had the beginnings of a modest community.

Many environmental problems stem from our unhealthy drive to get ahead as individuals in the world; at the same time that we want to get ahead, we remain isolated from the effects that our consumption and pollution have on the planet, on ourselves, and on our fellow humans. Yet the way we live has profound effects on our neighbors, both down the street and across the ocean. Since our lives are isolated from each other, it is easy not to realize that we may be hurting those around us. We live in a worldwide community, and we need to relearn the art of being good neighbors.

Living in community is something that Christ calls us to do, but it is not easy by any means. I was a resident assistant on the second floor of Mac-Evans during my junior and senior years, and became very conscious of how important it is to live in community well. My floor had about fifty guys but only one, community bathroom facility. Imagine how miserable the year would have been if everyone had just focused on themselves and had ignored those around them.

By the grace of God, we had a terrific floor of guys both years. Still, a good community does not mean a perfect one, and we often had to work out what it meant to live together. For instance, we established that if you cause the toilet to overflow (these things happen), then you should get some help and clean it up. If not, everyone else who walks into the bathroom gets their socks soaked in the mess, and the resident assistant misses his much-anticipated Sunday afternoon nap cleaning up after you.

Similarly we clarified that if you need to use the toilet, you should use *the toilet*. Windows do not make good substitutes; what goes out your window often comes in through the window on the floor below. And once again, the resident assistant gets to clean up after you. Except this time he (I) is (was) less than happy about it.

One more example: if your stereo speakers are bigger than your fridge, and you turn up the music loud enough for someone at the far end of the hallway to sing along with his door closed, then it is probably too loud. Likewise, experience taught me that in order for us to build community, durians should not be opened and eaten in the building.

Such problems arise because of ignorance or from thinking more about ourselves than our neighbors. They get resolved when, living in community, we become more aware of our impact on those around us and change our lives to better reflect Christ's love, grace and humility. Consider Wendell Berry's definition of community, taken from his book *Sex, Economy, Freedom, and Community*:

> Community is a locally understood interdependence of local people, local culture, local economy, and local nature. . . . A community identifies itself by an understood mutuality of interest. But it lives and acts by the common virtues of trust, goodwill, forbearance, self-restraint, compassion, and forgiveness. . . . Such a com-

munity has the power... to enforce decency without litigation. It has the power, that is, to influence behavior.[1]

Developing greater community with those around us, and with those who are affected by our way of living, is critical to resolving many of our environmental issues today. All the virtues that Berry mentions are often painfully absent from the accepted way in which our society functions. There are many ways we can improve. Building greater community will help bring these areas out of our blind spots and into our field of vision. Living in this community will motivate us to make the necessary changes so that we become a lesser part of the problem.

Another good aspect of living in community is that it allows us to work together to make a difference bigger than what we could do on our own. I remember many great examples from my floor, such as when a floor mate had some valuables stolen. The rest of us were able to chip in a little bit and help replace what was taken. It was a small sacrifice for each of us, but it added up to a big difference for our friend. Community empowers each of us to not only contribute less to the problem but to also work toward the solution with even greater effectiveness.

If community is so crucial to addressing our environmental concerns, it is also essential to develop within the creation-care movement itself. This was our primary reason for organizing the Wheaton Summit. We met together to worship, pray, fellowship, learn from existing efforts, encourage new ideas, and develop younger leadership. We gathered to start a community that will, we hope, become the start of a much bigger movement.

HANDS TO THE PLOW

The Wheaton Summit was an inspiring time of fellowship, and we were encouraged to hear about the creation-care efforts underway on many Christian campuses. At the same time, we were reminded of just how much room there is for growth.

Christian colleges and their students have a unique role to play in the crucial issue of creation care, because we are often the trendsetters in the Church. Christians tend to be a very cautious bunch; we need to be.

---

1. Wendell Berry, "Sex, Economy, Freedom, and Community," In *Sex, Economy, Freedom, and Community* (New York: Pantheon, 1993), 120.

Jesus often warned about being on constant lookout for false teachings, false prophets, and wolves dressed in sheep's clothing (Matt 7:15).

As we grapple with contemporary issues and moral problems like global warming and creation care, churches often look to Christian colleges and seminaries for wisdom and leadership. After all, these are the places where a great deal of the scholarship, writing, and organizing happens. That is why, for instance, it is significant that when the Evangelical Climate Initiative was released in early 2006, so many Christian college presidents had signed on.

Even so, Christian colleges remain far behind most of our secular counterparts in actively practicing creation care. Less than one-third of the member colleges of the Council of Christian Colleges and Universities have academic programs devoted to environmental study, and those that do often see the programs struggle from low enrollment. Many such campuses also do not have active environmental clubs or venues where people can discuss and practice creation care. Even colleges making good progress lack cross-campus communication and cooperation. Most student environmental groups still function as isolated and independent entities, having little impact outside of their communities.

Christian institutions like Wheaton need to take the lead and begin to change these problems. The role of students is especially important. College is our training ground; we are immersed in our studies and mentored by wise professors who then look to us to bring about change in the world. We are their investment for the kingdom and in the future, we will have the power to change our lifestyles, campuses, homes, churches, ministries, and communities. And after four years, waves upon waves of students go out from these institutions to make a difference for Christ. Let us not underestimate the influence of Christian colleges and their graduates.

This is why we are working to have student-led creation-care initiatives on every campus. Coming out of the summit, we also see the need for a student creation-care network that will continue to strengthen communication, cooperation, and community among student efforts on different campuses. Wheaton College has an ongoing role to play and can choose to be a student leader in this emerging movement. Wheaton is a well-known and highly respected institution to which many Christians already look for leadership. We hosted the Wheaton Summit on creation care and are the home of the first student chapter of A Rocha—Christians in Conservation, so we are off to a good start.

But this movement is far bigger than Wheaton College. The problems we face are much larger than any one individual or institution, and they will take all of us working together to solve. It starts personally with the most basic steps of switching to compact fluorescent light bulbs, traveling less, and taking shorter showers. But it continues with becoming involved on our campuses, in A Rocha student chapters, and as partners in other creation-care initiatives.

Caring for creation today is a big task, and our vision needs to be equally big. At times, it is easy to despair or to become frustrated with slow progress. Our eternal hope is Christ, but it's easy to wonder whether we actually stand a chance to make a difference in today's world. I am reminded of a quote from the recent film, *Amazing Grace*, where the young William Pitt advises his abolitionist friend, William Wilberforce: "We are too young to realize that certain things are impossible, so we'll do them anyway." There is truth to that assertion. They eventually succeeded in the work put before them and—by the grace of God—so will we.

9 · THE GREENING OF WHEATON COLLEGE: ENVIRONMENT, ECONOMICS, AND EQUITY

Vincent E. Morris

INTRODUCTION: A SYMBOLIC VEHICLE—GREEN FROM BROWN?

In the summer of 2003, a retired physician from Philadelphia named Dr. Ken Brown made an unusual donation offer to Gordon College in Wenham, Massachusetts.[1] Dr. Brown had been impressed with Gordon's interests in creation care, and especially with the efforts of one particular staff member, a carpenter and locksmith named Leo Cleary.

Leo had been a participant in Gordon's recent round-table discussions on waste removal and had been experimenting on his own in a college laboratory with ways to make biodiesel fuel out of waste cooking oil from the dining hall. Dr. Brown had happened on Leo and his experiments while visiting the campus as part of his service on Gordon College's President's Advisory Council.

Dr. Brown proposed to purchase on eBay and then donate to Gordon College a 1981 Volkswagen Rabbit diesel-powered automobile—if the college would agree to convert it into a biodiesel-using demonstration vehicle, testing Leo's simple method for making cheap, renewable fuel. Gordon accepted, and Leo flew to Ohio to drive the vehicle back to campus. Leo made the conversion and also built an inexpensive filter system to create biodiesel fuel out of waste cooking oil.[2] Some Gordon art students repainted the car and added a sign dubbing the vehicle the "Clean Machine." It gets fifty miles per gallon and the exhaust has the faintly pleasant smell of distant French fries.

1. Adapted from the story as related by editor Pat McKay in *Stillpoint*, Gordon College's alumni magazine (Summer 2005, 16–18).

2. In a bit of ironic symmetry, the disposal cost for a drum of waste cooking oil at the time was $55. The price of a barrel of oil on the world market at that time also happened to be $55. Gordon College went from being a net payer to using internal consumption to produce savings at both ends of the trade.

The Boston media ate it up, photographing Leo and the car and reporting extensively on the experiment both in print and on television. The positive publicity for Gordon was enormous, and was accented by other references to ancillary stewardship activities that Gordon undertakes.

In the summer of 2005, the Advancement Department at Wheaton College in Wheaton, Illinois, received a telephone call from a certain retired physician from Philadelphia who had an unusual proposal. The good Dr. Brown was apparently offering to donate a vintage Volkswagen Rabbit diesel automobile (he was in the process of bidding on this vehicle in an eBay auction) if someone from Wheaton would drive down to Effingham, Illinois, to pick up the vehicle if Brown won the bidding. The only string attached to the donation was that Dr. Brown wanted someone from Wheaton to convert the car to operate on biodiesel as an example of an alternatively powered vehicle.

After internal conversations between Advancement, Physical Plant, Geology, Biology, Physics, Risk Management, and other departments at Wheaton College, the good doctor's offer was declined—no one could be found at Wheaton College with the combined authority and interest to act on Dr. Brown's proposal.

THE GREENING OF WHEATON COLLEGE: GREEN FROM ORANGE?

Suggesting that Wheaton College is in the process of "greening" begs a question: what color has the college been all along?[3] The athletic teams wear uniforms in dark blue and orange, which are also the colors used in college logos and are even sported by the umbrellas in the outdoor café. Green, however, is not a color associated with most Wheaton College activities. Efforts to "green" the campus have seemed as isolated, weak, and as unlikely to succeed as a small reserve kicker wearing a green jersey in a milling sea of orange-clad football teammates.

"Greening" in this case is the idea of developing a campus environment conscious of creation-care obligations and seeking to operate in a

---

3. My wife is a talented artist. Many humorous conversations have taken place between us concerning colors, their names, functions, and attributes. While she continuously attempts to educate me on the intricacies of "mauve," "taupe," "fuchsia," and other entries in Crayola's "Big 64" box, my visual and descriptive spectrum is generally limited to the small box of eight—the ROY G. BIV rainbow selection of red, orange, yellow, green, blue, indigo, and violet; and I am a bit tentative about those last two.

sustainable way. While it should be noted that "sustainability" is an overworked and often poorly defined concept, the general theory (that humans owe a debt to our descendents to leave them with a set of resources necessary and helpful for their existence similar to or better than the set we received from our parents) is not usually questioned. Environmental movements often note that "we did not just receive the planet from our parents; we are borrowing it from our children and must return it in good condition."

Christians have a theological perspective on this concept. We believe God created all things and is in the process of reconciling *all things* to himself (Col 1:20). "Sustainability" to a Christian is living a life that honors the Creator by loving and caring for his creation as he does. For a Christian, the "greening" process is part of sanctification, the process of making holy all aspects of our lives. The challenge at Wheaton is how to incorporate this aspect of our faith into the things we do every day.

Missions, evangelism, academic excellence, student ministries, and successful athletics have been priorities at Wheaton for a long time, but creation-care initiatives have simply not been in the playbook for the administration, the employees, or the students. To change at this point—to develop a different campus culture—is difficult. "Greening" implies both that Wheaton is not currently green, and that the college is in the process of becoming more so. These statements are each true; the process of change is slow, moving through several shades on the color gradient toward green.

While some other schools were hiring full-time sustainability coordinators, sponsoring student energy-use-reduction competitions, constructing net-energy- or net-carbon-neutral residence halls, or composting dining hall waste, Wheaton focused elsewhere. While some other schools were seeking grants for expanded recycling programs, moving to nontoxic cleaning chemicals, planting tallgrass prairie instead of grass that requires mowing and watering, or purchasing energy from renewable sources, Wheaton weighed options. Not only were no rapid changes being made, but few official conversations seemed to be happening about possible stewardship change. Rather than green, one might say that Wheaton was the indeterminate gray of a battleship—and as difficult to turn.

WHY SHOULD CHRISTIANS CARE ABOUT ENVIRONMENTAL ISSUES?

Why isn't Wheaton greener? Actually, this is not too surprising. Although Wheaton College is part of the higher-education community that in general has been moving toward forms of sustainability, the college is embedded within North American evangelicalism, which in general has *not* been concerned about sustainability issues.

One of the larger theological puzzles of the late twentieth century was the conspicuous absence of evangelical Christians from mass involvement in and leadership of environmental stewardship movements in the United States. While much of the world, especially the developed nations, has been engaged for some time in discussion and proposals for action about the proper role of humans in relation to the environment, declining species, human-caused carbon-dioxide emissions, pollution, and similar concerns, Christianity has not presented a united front. Evangelicals in particular have been deeply divided on, and often completely absent from, the debates. It is not entirely clear why this should be the case.

I was interested enough by this puzzle that in 2001 I set out to write a master's thesis at Wheaton College Graduate School on this topic. After researching for a rather unexpected five years, I have learned many things.

WHAT I LEARNED, AND WHAT I DID WITH IT

I quickly learned that dramatic changes have been taking place in the early twenty-first century, during which time 1) the secular culture has made significant movement toward engagement with environmental concerns, and 2) a growing group of evangelicals and their institutions have made strong new commitments to creation-care efforts, sometimes in the face of intramural opposition.

It is not that Christians think the rest of God's creation is unimportant. Christians throughout history have understood that we learn about who God is from what he has made, as well as from what he does and tells us about himself. This is sometimes called the "Two-Books" understanding of God's revelation. Wheaton College's own Statement of Faith includes a paragraph reading, "WE BELIEVE that God has revealed Himself and His truth in the created order, in the Scriptures, and supremely in Jesus

Christ . . . ,"[4] intentionally including "the created order" as a source of revelation. As many Christian environmentalists have argued, how can we say we love God the Creator if we do not care for his creation?

But there is more to creation care than a pleasant background absorption of God's revelation. According to Genesis 1:26–28, humans are created "in the image of God" and called to express that image through caring for the creation as God does. It is not accidental that God placed Adam and Eve in a garden to care for it, to "tend and keep" it: this mission is similar to the modern police department's commitment, articulated in painted letters on a police cruiser door panel: "To Protect And To Serve." To be a human is to have responsibilities as a caretaker of creation. Given this clarion call to stewardship, why have Christians been reluctant to lead creation-care initiatives?

There are at least four main reasons evangelicals have often shied away from environmental movements, even when our theology might lead us to be involved. These reasons are 1) a belief that the environment is not in crisis and not in need of our special considerations; 2) an eschatological belief system that indicates the earth and everything in it will burn up and is destined to be destroyed; 3) concerns that involvement in environmental movements leads to a dangerous compromise with pantheistic and paganistic ideas that dilute and destroy the gospel message; and 4) a sense that environmental concerns are real but are far less important or deserving of attention than missions and evangelism.

1) *The environment isn't really in crisis*

Some Christians do not think the environment is something to worry about. This group's membership may be shrinking in the face of accumulating firsthand evidence of environmental problems. Christian environmental scientist Calvin DeWitt describes seven specific "degradations of creation" that he believes are clearly happening and are caused by humans:

1) Alteration of planetary energy exchange with the Sun, including global warming and ozone shield depletion;

---

4. Quoted verbatim from the Wheaton College Statement of Faith. Accessed February 10, 2008. Online: http://www.wheaton.edu/welcome/aboutus_mission.html.

2) Land degradation through erosion, salinization, and desertification, including through conversion of land use from forests and crops to urban uses;

3) Deforestation, resulting in degraded soil and "diminished biodiversity;"

4) Species extinction "on a scale similar to the greatest extinction episodes in the Earth's geological history," caused mainly by destruction of habitat, urban development, and agricultural use of modern seed and livestock varieties;

5) Water degradation through pollution and leaching of wastes;

6) Global toxification due to worldwide contamination via 70,000 manmade chemicals, the "products and by-products of human activity;"

7) Human and cultural degradation in which cultures that have "learned to live sustainably on earth" are either extinguished or threatened.

DeWitt further states, "We are discovering that the common agent of creation's degradation is human action."[5] James Nash agrees:

> [T]he ecological crisis is definitely dangerous. The scale and scope of the problems are severe . . . [W]ith vast human populations wielding awesome technological tools, the crisis is developing rapidly, often radically, and sometimes irreversibly. The planet and its diverse populations of species are in peril, poisoned and impoverished on a score of fronts simultaneously. Ecological problems are serious and persistent, and the appropriate responses from Christians and other citizens should be correspondingly serious and persistent. The ecological crisis warrants a prime place on the Christian moral and political agenda, ranking with the quest for economic justice and international peace.[6]

It is becoming more and more difficult every day to assert that the environment does not suffer from devastating human-caused problems.

---

5. As outlined by DeWitt in *Caring for Creation: Responsible Stewardship of God's Handiwork. With responses by Richard A. Baer, Jr., Thomas Sieger Derr, and Vernon J. Ehlers.* Kuyper Lecture for the Center for Public Justice (Grand Rapids: Baker, 1998), 17–19, and often expressed by DeWitt elsewhere.

6. James Nash, *Loving Nature: Ecological Integrity and Christian Responsibility* (Nashville: Abingdon, 1991), 24.

2) Everything's going to burn up anyway

Another set of Christians may not be interested in being part of creation-care activities because they genuinely believe the Earth will be completely destroyed soon. This view draws support from scriptural passages such as Revelation 21:1 ("Then I saw a new heaven and a new earth, for the first heaven and the first earth had passed away, and there was no longer any sea.") or 2 Peter 3:8, 10, 12–13 ("By the same word the present heavens and earth are reserved for fire. . . . But the day of the Lord will come like a thief. The heavens will disappear with a roar; the elements will be destroyed by fire, and the earth and everything in it will be laid bare . . . . That day will bring about the destruction of the heavens by fire, and the elements will melt in the heat. But in keeping with his promise we are looking forward to a new heaven and a new earth, the home of righteousness." [NIV]).

Eschatology determines ethics. If Christians believe the earth will be destroyed soon, why spend effort on it? Who repairs the roof on a house slated for demolition next week?

But this may be an incorrect interpretation, both of the quoted passages and of eschatology. Particularly notable are the modern Bible translations' renderings of the Greek word in 2 Peter 3:10 of "disclosed" (NRSV) or "laid bare" (NIV) rather than older versions' "burned up" (e.g., KJV, ASV, NASB; intriguingly, the Vulgate's best manuscripts do not have the phrase including this word, while other lesser manuscripts have it with *exurentur*—"burned up/consumed"). This change makes a significant theological difference for the fate of the world, and by implication, for how humans should care for it. Wheaton College professor Douglas Moo notes that the translation "burned up" "is almost certainly incorrect. The text is notoriously difficult. . . . What it means is more difficult to determine, but perhaps the idea of being 'laid bare' before God for judgment is the best option."[7] In this interpretation of Scripture, especially in

---

[7] From Douglas J. Moo, "Nature in the New Creation: New Testament Eschatology and the Environment." *Journal of the Evangelical Theological Society,* 49 (2006) 449–88. See also Gale Z. Heide, "What Is New about the New Heaven and the New Earth? A Theology of Creation From Revelation 21 and 2 Peter 3." *Journal of the Evangelical Theological Society* 40 (1997), 37–56. Heide concludes that the apocalyptic language of Revelation and Peter is not meant to imply a literal destruction of matter, that the creation has a future, and that humans therefore have a stewardship mandate to care for that which God intends to redeem (55–56).

light of Colossians 1:20 and Romans 8:28, it seems that the fate of creation is to be purified, redeemed, and renewed—not destroyed. Maybe we should fix that roof after all.

3) Fear of paganism, nature worship and panentheism

Another reason Christians are skeptical of environmental initiatives is out of concern that such efforts are idolatrous, leading to worship of the creation instead of the Creator. Some Christians have (often rightly) associated various environmental conservation movements with pantheism or other non-Christian views that too greatly exalt the Earth, and therefore have shunned involvement with them. Christian fears are suspicious of theological syncretism lurking in environmental movements. Such movements often seek ethical foundations in a variety of religions, using language that seems similar in appearance but can be quite different in substance from Christian orthodoxy. For example, in an influential article, Rev. Vincent Rossi wrote:

> We must love nature for herself and also because she is a "handmaiden" of the Lord. We must return to a kind of *aboriginal* consciousness of nature, an atonement of nature so direct one could not open the earth or cut down a tree or kill an animal without a profound emotional response or a heartfelt prayer. Our awareness of nature must be directly attached to our own feelings, as it once was for primitive man. Nature is a theophany. Man must learn once again to see God everywhere in Nature. We must let the scales fall from our eyes, and discerning the Divine Presence in all things, love the earth and all nature as the visible Form of God.[8]

Such near deification of nature—along with theologically charged phrases such as "theophany" and "discerning the Divine Presence in all things"—rides a line perilously close to panentheism.[9] Perhaps instructive here is the following statement from John Calvin:

---

8. Vincent Rossi, "The Eleventh Commandment: Toward an Ethic of Ecology," *Epiphany Journal* 1 (1981) 3–19 (emphasis original).

9. Both pantheism and panentheism are here understood as anti-Christian positions. The material universe is not to be equated with God (pantheism), nor is every aspect of the universe pervaded with "God-ness" (panentheism). Pantheism is clearly in opposition to Christianity, and one of the dangers of environmental movements for Christians

> I admit, indeed, that the expression, "Nature is God," may be piously used, if dictated by a pious mind; but as it is inaccurate and harsh (Nature being more properly the order which has been established by God), in matters which are so very important, and in regard to which special reverence is due, it does harm to confound the Deity with the inferior operations of his hands.[10]

In addition to the theological concerns, practical suspicions also abound. Sometimes it seems that even the most innocent Christian approach to creation-care quickly expands into conflation and entanglement with other issues: antiwar or antinuclear sentiment, solutions to poverty, the role of women in developing societies, vegetarianism, and other issues—all gathered loosely under the broad tent of "environmentalism."

As an example of this conflation, the list of exhibitors at the 2005 Midwest Renewable Energy Fair held in Custer, Wisconsin,[11] included booths for many of the expected solar- and wind-power installers alongside organic food producers; handmade-soap makers; the Clearwater Folk School; the Modern Homesteading Movement; ambassadors for indigenous Amazonian herbal remedies; experts in socially and environmentally responsible investing; representatives from both *The Nation* and *Mother Jones* magazines; members of Deeply Rooted ("A forming intentional community based on earth centered [sic] spirituality and sustainable living."); members of Nukewatch ("A peace and environmental group dedicated to abolishing militarism, weapons of mass destruction and nuclear power."); representatives of the Church of Deep Ecology, of Windy City Hemp, and of the Wisconsin Interfaith Climate and Energy Campaign. A "peace walk" and yoga classes were also available. The connection of some of these ideas to renewable energy seems rather distant indeed.

---

is an insidious, creeping panentheism. The ideas that God is Creator and Sustainer and cares for and values his creation, and that creation has intrinsic value, are eminently Christian, while the idea that every bush and tree has an infusion of God (wood sprites and water spirits, etc.) is not. The latter fails to make a sufficient ontological distinction between the Creator and the creation, although it is not full-blown pantheism.

10. John Calvin, *Institutes of the Christian Religion,* trans. Henry Beveridge (Grand Rapids: Eerdmans, 1975), I.v.v.

11. Accessed June 2005. Online: http://www.the-mrea.org/fair_workshops.php.

4) Higher priorities: save souls, not whales

There are many causes in which Christians can and do involve themselves in the name of the faith. For those who feel that Christians should express interest in or care for the environment, it is not enough simply to note that in the current era many persons feel that the environment warrants special concern. Competing claims abound for time, money, and support. If care for the environment is to take a place on the list of Christian concerns, elbow room must be found among standard, long-term Christian interests such as missions and evangelistic efforts to spread the gospel, the plight of the poor, and the constant struggle for theological or cultural purity. In the Christian drive to "save the lost," the push to "save the whales" may not resonate as an established priority: whale calls may be drowned out by altar calls in the summons for Christian attention.[12]

In his famous and repeatedly cited article in 1967, Lynn White argued that it was in the very nature of Christian theology to have no care for the Earth.[13] White notes that some Christians interpreted the concept that humans are made "in God's image" as a license for humankind to dominate the rest of creation not so made: "No new set of basic values has been accepted in our society to displace those of Christianity. Hence we shall continue to have a worsening ecological crisis until we reject the Christian axiom that nature has no reason for existence save to serve man." This is a harsh rejection of Christian theology's ability to manage environmental crises. The antidote is to realize that part of what it means to be God's regent on earth is not that nature serves us, but that we serve it.

There are many parts of the world in which caring for creation is inextricably tied to care for people. To gain an audience, pastors and missionaries must address real, felt needs. In these places, environmental issues are intimately intertwined with issues of poverty and social justice—accepted Christian concerns of long standing. To attempt to solve environmental problems without tackling the deep-seated underlying social issues (e.g., land distribution, women's rights, fair laws and admin-

---

12. The whales, in fact, have been saved. While the blue and bowhead whales are still endangered, the minke, for instance, is so common one bureaucrat from Japan (one of the few nations, along with Norway and Iceland, that hunts whales on a significant scale) called them the "cockroaches of the sea" ("A bloody war," *The Economist*, January 3, 2004, 56–58).

13. Lynn White Jr. "The Historical Roots of Our Ecological Crisis," *Science* 155 (1967) 1203–6.

istrative justice, and economic problems such as education, health care, and adequate fuel distribution) is an exercise in futility.

In September 2004 mudslides and flooding in Haiti killed over one thousand people when rains from Hurricane Jeanne undermined soil on slopes denuded of trees by a populace desperate for cooking fuel. The residents of Haiti cut down the trees on their island not because they don't know that this practice causes soil erosion and loss of fertility; they cut down trees because they have *no other resources* for obtaining fuel, and trees can be used to make a bit of charcoal to cook a meal. Similar scenarios have played out in Honduras, Guatemala, and other impoverished areas. To serve Christ and his kingdom, Christians must understand that sometimes prioritizing for people can only be accomplished through creation-care activities that nurture those people.

CARING FOR CREATION: GREEN VS. RED

Given this daunting list of reasons Christians can give *not* to be involved in environmental initiatives, in spite of the counterarguments, one can see why some at Wheaton College, or elsewhere too, might not think creation care is particularly important. Ernst Conradie summarizes the problem:

> A Christian environmental ethos, praxis and spirituality requires theological reflection on the convictions, beliefs, stories, symbols, worldviews, values, traditions, rituals, institutions and religious experiences that may support it. Indeed, why should Christians *as Christians* engage in earthkeeping in the first place? Despite the wealth of literature in ecological theology, there is still a lack of clarity on this very basic theological question.[14]

In Genesis 1:26–28, humans are given dominion over the rest of creation, which is implied to be wild and in need of a sort of taming. The role of humans is to continue the creative work of God by setting boundaries, creating gardens out of wilderness, and exercising all the powers of a steward and caretaker to determine what parts of the creation will thrive

---

14. Ernst Conradie, "An Agenda for Ecological Theology," in *Biodiversity and Ecology: An InterDisciplinary Challenge*, ed. Denis Edwards and Mark Worthing (Adelaide: Australian Theological Forum, 2004), 19.

and which will be restrained. Nature is indeed red in tooth and claw;[15] humans serve a dual role as nurturer and restrainer of nature's forces. In a very real sense, being made in God's image gives us his authority to continue his creative acts, saying to the natural world, as God did, "Thus far you come, and no farther" (Job 38:11, ESV).

My father, ever the farmer and gardener, expresses this in a very practical and nonacademic way: "A weed is a plant out of place." Given that the weed is such, the gardener-steward reserves the right—and has the duty—to remove or destroy the weed in one place, where it might be preserved and nourished as a favored plant just a few garden rows away. Proper stewardship is not nature worship, nor is it destructive assertion of human dominion. It is firm caretaking that can only be done out of a thoughtful deliberation for what God would want us to do, for how our actions affect the rest of creation, including other humans, and through a humble self-denial at times.

It is this proper understanding of the Christian's role as steward—one of thoughtful deliberation and the weighing and balancing of priorities—that must guide Wheaton College's deliberations on what it means to become greener. It is critical to note that the role of gardener and creation caretaker is riddled with difficult decisions and compromises.

INTERVIEW WITH DR. LITFIN: BLUE, NOT GREEN

As I wandered the silent and dusty halls of academic arcana, reading and writing for my thesis in theology, at one point I researched the official statements made by many evangelical schools and denominations concerning creation care. Wheaton College's Statement of Faith received the same scrutiny, and I learned it actually says little on the subject. Wheaton has intentionally avoided taking official positions on certain controversial issues on which Christians of goodwill find themselves divided, such as the proper mode of baptism, glossolalia (speaking in tongues) in worship, or even abortion. No phrase or position statement on any of these or on several other fractious topics appears in Wheaton's Statement. It references creation care only in the following paragraph:

---

15. "Who trusted God was love indeed / And love Creation's final law / Tho' Nature, red in tooth and claw / With ravine, shriek'd against his creed . . . " *(In Memoriam A.H.H.,* by Alfred Lord Tennyson [Canto 56], 1849).

> WE BELIEVE that the one, holy, universal Church is the body of Christ and is composed of the communities of Christ's people. The task of Christ's people in this world is to be God's redeemed community, embodying His love by worshipping God with confession, prayer, and praise; by proclaiming the gospel of God's redemptive love through our Lord Jesus Christ to the ends of the earth by word and deed; *by caring for all of God's creation* and actively seeking the good of everyone, especially the poor and needy.[16]

Although it is nice to see this acknowledgement in the Statement of Faith, I wondered what it meant in practice. So in May of 2005 I requested and was granted a brief interview with Wheaton College president, Dr. Duane Litfin. I wished to ask him a handful of questions about what he felt were Wheaton College's stewardship and creation-care responsibilities.

In the course of our conversation, Dr. Litfin indicated that stewardship issues were not a high priority to him or to the College: "Wheaton College has more to do than this." This was not a completely unexpected response; it fit into the last of the four main categories I had identified in my thesis as reasons that evangelicals have not joined environmental movements in strength. Dr. Litfin was interested neither in pushing a creation-care agenda nor in making "symbolic statements" about the environment, he said. Wheaton College simply had other, higher priorities than creation-care initiatives. I was not surprised at his answer; it was Reason No. 4 in my list of "Why Christians Don't Get Involved," and I had heard it plenty of times before.

But, I thought to myself as I walked away, *creation care is not like other kinds of theological positions*. We do not choose between it and other priorities. We each demonstrate a level of creation care—or lack of it—every day. We all must eat and use energy and get around (driving, walking, flying, biking) and generate trash. We "take a position" on creation care simply by living. We cannot remain neutral on the subject, as we might on the proper mode of baptism. Everything we do every day, personally and institutionally at the college, demonstrates our care for creation or our lack of it.

What is more, many stewardship failures result not only in negative effects on the planet, but in reduced health and quality of life for other

---

16. Accessed February 8, 2008. Online: http://www.wheaton.edu/welcome/aboutus_mission.html (emphasis added).

people elsewhere. If we make thoughtless choices resulting in wasteful energy-use, nonsustainable agricultural production, excessive material consumption, extravagant modes of travel and other similar decisions, we can have the effect of making the hard lives of others in the world even harder. This does not seem like a Christian thing to do to others.

Wheaton College should indeed maintain its historical emphasis on missions, evangelism, liberal-arts education, and the development of whole and effective Christians "for Christ and his kingdom." But the College should do so by means of activities, programs, and initiatives that also exemplify thoughtful creation care and deliberate stewardship to one another, to our students, and to the world.

I left the meeting in a blue, philosophical mood, slightly depressed about Wheaton College—soon to be my graduate alma mater—and the college's apparent lack of interest in environmental stewardship. But it would not be long before a new development arose.

ONE STUDENT, ONE SPEECH, ONE DIRECTIVE

That summer I heard through the grapevine that a student, Ben Lowe, had invited Dr. Litfin to speak at his Chinese Alliance Church at a seminar on creation care. Ben was a sharp and talented junior at the time, a student-leader who had worked with Dr. Fred Van Dyke to start the first-ever college chapter of the Christian environmental group A Rocha.[17] A Rocha Wheaton was sponsoring the seminar, and Dr. Litfin had agreed to be a speaker. I was intrigued to learn this. While Dr. Litfin is an excellent public speaker, my interview with him earlier that summer had not left me with the impression that Christian environmentalism was a topic on which he was well versed.

About that time I received an alumni magazine from Gordon College describing their biodiesel vehicle, Leo Cleary's Clean Machine. The magazine also listed several other stewardship initiatives that Gordon was undertaking. Clearly that school was finding ways to make creation

---

17. Named for the Portuguese phrase for "The Rock" and (I am told) pronounced to rhyme with "a pasha," A Rocha was founded by Peter and Miranda Harris, first as a "Christian Bird Observatory" in Portugal when no appropriate Christian service opportunities presented themselves in East Africa, their original missions destination. A Rocha's Web site can be found online at http://en.arocha.org/home/ (accessed February 2008).

care a priority in ways that Wheaton had not attempted. I forwarded a copy of the article to Dr. Litfin, suggesting that in light of his upcoming speech, he might appreciate some examples and resources on the topic. I also included the sad commentary that just as he had contacted Gordon, Dr. Brown had contacted Wheaton as well about a biodiesel purchase, and no one could take up Leo's banner here. Dr. Litfin returned a brief note of thanks, and I thought the matter was closed and returned to my thesis writing.

I did not attend the speech at the Chinese Alliance Church, but I heard it went well. Afterward I received a surprising note from Dr. Litfin, attached to a copy of the article with Leo's confident, beaming face. The small sticky note read only, *"To Vince: Talk to me about this."*

When I reached his office, Dr. Litfin got to the point quickly. He asked me directly, "What do you think Wheaton College should be doing on environmental issues?" I was somewhat taken aback, as I had not anticipated this question. However, I had been thinking about it for quite some time beforehand, so I responded, "Wheaton College could be doing many things. But what we need most, and first, is what I would call a *locus of conversation*—a way to talk among ourselves about what we could do and should do about creation care." I knew several employees who wished to do more but felt helpless and disconnected. The Purchasing director wanted to use more recycled paper in copiers but wasn't sure others would be satisfied. The Physical Plant director and the Auto Shop mechanics had separately expressed interest in alternatively fueled vehicles, but they weren't sure if Purchasing would go for that. I had heard many similar conversations, but there was no place to have them together to figure out a way forward. "That's what we need: a place to talk among ourselves about appropriate stewardship actions the College should take."

Dr. Litfin responded, "I agree. We need an Environmental Stewardship Advisory Committee. I want you to start it and be the chair. It will report directly to me—an audience of one. It should be composed of Wheaton College staff members rather than faculty, because I need people who will salute." Dr. Litfin assigned three tasks to the committee:

1) Assess what the College is doing, and how we are doing on environmental stewardship issues.
2) Seek good ideas for best practices and improvements.
3) Present these ideas and request resources to make them happen.

Thus did the first official new leaves burst forth in the greening of Wheaton College, through the formation of a new Environmental Stewardship Advisory Committee—"ESAC" for short.

Shortly after, Dr. Litfin took the bold and personally costly step of being one of the first eighty-four signatories on the Evangelical Climate Initiative's "Climate Change: An Evangelical Call To Action,"[18] calling for a "focus on such matters as energy efficiency, the use of renewable energy, low carbon dioxide-emitting technologies, and the purchase of hybrid vehicles" and pledging "to act on the basis of the claims made in this document. We will not only teach the truths communicated here but also seek ways to implement the actions that follow from them. In the name of Jesus Christ our Lord, we urge all who read this declaration to join us in this effort." At least one Wheaton College trustee, I learned, questioned this act by the president. Another group of evangelicals published a counterstatement, saying that the first statement shouldn't have been signed at all, by anyone. Evangelicalism suddenly found itself at odds internally, debating what shade of green is best.

As one who believes "green" has been sorely neglected in the Christian color scheme, all this change and potential change at Wheaton was very encouraging—except that as the new ESAC chair, I needed some good ideas about how to begin.

THE FORMATION OF ESAC

Fortunately for me, Dr. Fred van Dyke of Wheaton College's Environmental Studies Department[19] had previously proposed to the faculty of Wheaton College that such a committee be formed. The faculty had voted against Fred's proposal for creating a standing committee, citing (among other reasons) a desire to prevent a proliferation of official college committees. However, Fred generously forwarded to me his draft documents

---

18. Accessed February 10, 2008. Online: http://www.christiansandclimate.org/statement

19. "Dr. Van Dyke is also known for his leadership in Christian environmental stewardship. He is senior author of *Redeeming Creation: The Biblical Basis for Environmental Stewardship* (InterVarsity Press) and a former educational consultant to the Pew Charitable Trust's Global Stewardship Initiative for the development of environmental studies programs in colleges of the Counsel [sic] for Christian Colleges and Universities," according to the Wheaton College Environmental Studies departmental Web site at http://www.wheaton.edu/envstudies/people.html, accessed February 11, 2008.

covering the formation and function of an environmental stewardship committee, and we were able to craft a committee of several interested persons who all volunteered their time to serve:

- Tony Dawson, Assistant Business Manager
- Greg Doty, Director of Purchasing
- Dr. P. J. Hill, Professor of Economics
- Jim Johnson, Director of Physical Plant
- Ben Lowe, Wheaton senior and leader of A Rocha, student environmental group
- Bruce Koenigsberg, architect in Campus Planning
- Steve Mead, Business Manager
- Vince Morris, Director of Risk Management (Chair)
- Bruce Norquist, Residence Life
- Lisa Richmond, College Librarian
- Dr. Fred van Dyke, Professor of Environmental Studies

In this initial assemblage we did stretch Dr. Litfin's directives somewhat by including two faculty members.[20] ESAC was formed largely along the lines of Dr. Van Dyke's initial proposal. He and his like-minded colleagues deserve significant credit for this contribution to community life and policy at Wheaton. We also added a student member, Ben Lowe, who I felt earned a membership through his leadership of A Rocha Wheaton, his invitation to the president to speak at the Chinese Alliance Church, and his general good sense and hard work on creation-care issues. It was a fortunate and prophetic choice.

HOW TO BEGIN: THEOLOGY, PRACTICALITY, CHANGE

After a preliminary meeting or two in which we heard instructions from Dr. Litfin concerning our three tasks, the first item ESAC took up was

20. Like Hawkeye Pierce and B. J. Hunnicut, the skilled and sarcastic physicians from M.A.S.H. (http://www.mash4077.co.uk/index.php, accessed February 10, 2008), these faculty members might not be trusted to salute properly, but their respective expertise was important to the group. Dr. Van Dyke's thoughtful contributions extend far beyond the formative documents and ideas he provided, and Dr. Hill has written extensively on the economic aspects of certain environmental initiatives. On occasion, Dr. Hill's perspectives on the efficacy—or lack thereof—of proposed stewardship initiatives led me to dub him "the loyal opposition." His contributions are essential for an honest weighing of the costs of certain activities, a constant reminder of the tradeoffs that must be made.

the development of a theological statement, a rationale for the use of our time and effort on creation-care issues. Many such statements exist for evangelical denominations and organizations, so we were not exactly starting from scratch. However, Wheaton has not historically expressed a theological position on creation care, and any such statement would necessarily be subject to considerable scrutiny. It was not a task to be taken up lightly, and the committee felt the weight. Nevertheless we agreed that we needed the biblical and theological basis in place to guide our future decision making.

After much conversation within the committee and further consultation with theologians from Wheaton College's graduate school, a satisfactory draft was composed. It emphasizes the call we have from God for proper stewardship of his creation, grounded in the promise that Christ has come to reconcile all things to himself, including both humans and the rest of the created order. We are called to exert our influence toward stewardship and toward the right reflection of God's intention for redemption. (See Appendix A). This draft was submitted to Dr. Litfin for consideration and is still pending as of the time of this writing. In the meantime, ESAC has been operating under the assumption that this or a similar statement provides our rationale.

The second major task for ESAC was to develop a matrix for decision making. How could we report to Dr. Litfin what Wheaton College "is currently doing" about the environment, much less determine what we "should" be doing about environmental stewardship, if we could not weigh the relative benefits and costs of possible decisions on creation-care actions? And this is only possible if we have a priority system, a grid through which to sift our options.

After some discussion, ESAC determined that a reasonable approach to creation-care decisions for Wheaton College might be summarized as *"minimizing the* overall *costs of our actions."* This specifically and intentionally includes the costs to others of the actions of Wheaton College. For example, we wish to consider not only the direct costs of, for instance, electricity we use that is produced by burning coal at a power plant, but also the indirect and diffuse costs of marginally increased childhood asthma or damaging atmospheric pollution incurred as a result of the college's choice to use electricity produced in this way.

Thus the college's stewardship decisions should consider not only costs to ourselves but also the effects of those decisions on others. These latter effects and costs admittedly are often quite difficult to measure, but they are nonetheless real and perhaps avoidable. It seems to ESAC that the Christlike approach to a decision must include consideration of these external costs borne by others, which should be minimized at least as much as our own internal financial costs. Thus the group developed the beginnings of a *cost-minimizing* decision matrix (Appendix B). It is a set of questions that could be applied to decisions with demonstrable environmental impact, beginning with a need the college community has and considering ways to meet that need that minimize overall costs.

A complementary approach is to attempt to *minimize consumption* at all levels. While this approach does not explicitly consider impacts on others, it does define reduction of internal costs and concomitant reduction of demand on the environment by the college as worthy goals. Steve Mead helped the committee by presenting this *consumption-minimizing* approach as a set of questions (Appendix C) matching those of the cost-minimization approach. These two sets of questions are necessarily works in progress; a college policy statement on seeking creation-care options in decision making might best combine elements of the two.

LEVERS OF POWER AND INFLUENCE

It soon became clear to ESAC that if we recommended changes for college activities to be greener, there were only a few "levers" we could pull to make our case. We decided we had four main ways to effect change:

Economic: Make something cheaper, and people will naturally gravitate toward it instead of alternatives. Unfortunately, at Wheaton there were not many obvious choices for encouraging creation-care changes through economics. Most easy economic fixes had already been instituted on their own merits, regardless of environmental effects. This continues to pose a challenge to the committee, as part of our instructions from Dr. Litfin were to "look for payback." We were instructed to propose net-neutral projects, and that payback terms should target less than five years. This is a steep hill to climb for stewardship investments.

Mandated: Forced compliance was not something we felt was realistic in many areas, whether it be staff paper recycling or student hot-water shower time limits. Our motivational levers will need to be other approaches most of the time.

Educative: Sometimes people change their behavior simply because they learn of a better alternative. Although this doesn't work for entrenched behaviors like smoking, we could think of several areas where an educational campaign was likely to be successful in motivating the campus community to change certain behaviors. We began planning some recommendations for educational opportunities, like a Sustainability Day event.

Moral: If people become convinced that a certain behavior is wrong, they will often refrain from it even if it is cheaper and voluntary. This is the strongest of the four motivators if the lever is pulled, because it reaches deep into the heart of the person to draw power from what he or she believes in.

The strongest argument ESAC has for promoting change is the moral one. It seems immoral and un-Christlike for Wheaton College, or anyone else, to push off costs we should pay ourselves onto others as externalities, once we know about them and less externally-costly alternatives.

To use a (mostly) hypothetical example, if we 1) purchase electricity at three cents per kilowatt from coal-fired power plants in Gary, Indiana, and thus incrementally increase the known rate of childhood asthma caused by emissions in that region, and if we 2) could purchase (or generate) electricity from renewable sources for five cents per kilowatt, what is our moral responsibility? Clearly we live in a fallen world and cannot avoid making sinful choices or having sinful impacts on others, but "stewardship" is not only financial. Can we live with the 40 percent "savings" on electricity produced by our deliberate choice to inflict our cost as an externality of additional illness in children? Is this a fair comparison of stewardship options? Is it trite to ask "What would Jesus have us do?" about such situations? What constitutes "good stewardship" and a "good witness"? Is it right to choose the cheaper power source if the children don't know their increased asthma is partly my fault? And probably sometime in their lives, these children will do something that pushes some external costs onto me; is that a fair tradeoff that allows me to continue my tit-for-future-tat behavior?

ESAC continued to identify ways Wheaton could become greener, weighing how to do so against the costs of doing so. ESAC has no budget and no authority to mandate change; however, one interesting outgrowth of ESAC's activities and conversations is the awareness that although ESAC is charged with making recommendations only, certain purchases, changes in policy, and other decisions are likely to take place organically simply because they seem like good ideas to the committee members *who happen to be in charge of that aspect of college operations.* These sorts of decisions are not likely to wait on administrative policy where such policy is currently silent.

In the meantime, through these slow and cautious deliberations, one ESAC member at least was not standing pat. Ben Lowe had big plans.

THE WHEATON SUMMIT, JANUARY 2007:
GREENING AMIDST THE WHITE

One of the most hopeful signs of the greening of Wheaton was not really the work of ESAC at all. In January 2007 A Rocha Wheaton, the highly talented student group led by Ben Lowe, worked in conjunction with the Center for Applied Christian Ethics (CACE) to focus campus attention on environmental stewardship issues, particularly on climate change concerns. Sir John Houghton, an evangelical Christian and arguably the world's leading climate change expert, spoke on several occasions to the student body and other groups. During one of the snowiest, most frigid periods that Chicago had experienced in years, students from A Rocha Wheaton sponsored a gathering of students from other schools, including from Gordon College and John Brown University.

The combined assembly spent several days in worship and conversation about ways to promote various stewardship initiatives, learning from each other and hearing stories of incremental campus transformations. It required some imagination to discuss climate change, hustling through white flakes with frosty breath hanging in the air. But the very fact that staid Wheaton College was hosting such an event was historic for many. We at Wheaton learned that we are by no means the leading school among our peers in this arena. Many schools are "greener."

Some schools sent only one or two student representatives in fledgling efforts, while others sent large contingents of students and faculty or staff, fresh from implementing yet another stewardship effort. Gordon

College students told of their fine recycling program, while Eastern College representatives described their 100-percent wind-powered campus. The students spent time in prayer for God's guidance on how to implement stewardship efforts that would best fulfill his will for the reconciliation of all things to himself. Presumably on their campuses they are now wrestling with which sustainability projects to recommend first—at least that's what ESAC did after the summit.

NEXT STEPS?

Once the Environmental Stewardship Advisory Committee had established both a theological basis and a matrix for appropriate decision making, we deliberated concerning which stewardship ideas should be examined first. There was a long list, ranging from the immediately plausible to the far reaching. Some of the options for consideration included

- Transportation
    - Hybrid vehicles
    - Electric vehicles
    - Car pooling and/or vehicle- and parking-minimization incentives
- New construction/renovation—what does "green" mean here? LEEDS certification?
- Water use
- Energy use and sourcing: solar, wind, geothermal, etc.; automatic off-switches, timers
- Food waste-reduction and disposal
- Food purchase impacts—effects on soil, farming techniques, effects on people producing the food
- Pesticide/herbicide/fertilizer use
- Chemical waste stream (e.g., consider microchemistry?)
- Sourcing of products:
    - Recycled source
    - Ethical/organic sources (e.g., coffee)
    - Local purchases?
    - Selection of materials (e.g., steel, concrete, etc.) based on long-term impact

- Waste stream: life cycle of computers, etc.
- Paper use
- Science Station as appropriate technologies construction site
  - Wind
  - Solar
  - Earth-sheltered
- Vermiculture
- Biodiesel usage
- Mulching/composting
- Biological pest control
- Gray water recycling
- Rainwater capture and storage
- Rooftop gardens
- Capturing SRC exercise-machine energy
- Controlling "light pollution" (viz. astronomy) with directed shields for night lights, etc.

Eventually three subcommittees were formed, to examine "How We Eat," "How We Construct," and "How We Get Around." Subsequently other subcommittees examined questions such as "How We Use Paper" and "How We Use Energy." We chose these from the list because these specific areas are both common and largely unavoidable in our daily lives. Making good decisions on how to practice good stewardship in these areas will yield especially high long-term dividends.

By October of 2006, ESAC submitted our first annual report to Dr. Litfin. In it we recommended the adoption of a theological statement giving the rationale for concerted institutional stewardship efforts, and the adoption of a matrix for proper stewardship decision making. In addition, we made several specific recommendations for changes at Wheaton, some of which ESAC members had the authority to implement autonomously. Here is a sampling:

Alternative-Fuel Vehicle Expo: In both summer 2006 and spring 2007, the college hosted Alternative-Fuel Vehicle Expositions; vendors displayed several types of electric, hybrid, natural gas, and other vehicles. Public Safety took the recommendations of Purchasing, Physical Plant, and the Business Office and purchased a hybrid Ford Explorer as a patrol vehicle.

The Physical Plant Department recently purchased what is likely to be the first of several all-electric, plug-in work vehicles for the trades.

Residence hall utilities-usage competition: Devices are being installed in residence halls to host a per-pillow competition to encourage students to be aware of their energy and water use, and to reduce it.

Food-waste monitoring: Working with our campus food service, Bon Appétit, we are recommending a plotting graph near the dining hall exit as a lever to encourage students to waste less food.

Paper-use reduction: Copiers and printers have been set to two-sided printing as a default. Staff offices are slowly moving toward a paperless, scanned document system.

LEED-certified construction: The renovation of both the Memorial Student Center and the proposed new science building have sustainable construction (LEED-certified) points built into their specifications. The Physical Plant Department is examining options for obtaining electrical power from renewable sources. Energy-efficient lighting and low-flow shower heads have been installed throughout the campus. Professors staffing the Science Station in South Dakota have proposed that its next renovation plans include solar and wind facilities.

In the spring of 2007, citing the press of responsibilities, Dr. Litfin asked Senior Vice President Dr. David Johnston to take over direct supervision of ESAC. Ben Lowe graduated from Wheaton College and became a full-time staffer with A Rocha USA. In the summer of 2007, Dave accepted ESAC's fall 2006 recommendation to put an operations person in charge of the committee, with authority to take action on ideas—authority that Risk Management does not have. Can Wheaton be considered a "green" campus now? Not yet. We have a long way to go in some rather basic areas before we can begin to be proud of our progress. But we are moving forward at last. The best part is that we are doing so with great confidence that we have a group with authority to make creation-care recommendations, a good theological basis, a decision matrix to help with priorities, and some solid success stories from the last two years. This represents tremendous change from two years ago. It can no longer be said that Wheaton College ignores environmental issues. The greening of Wheaton College has begun.

CONCLUSION: ANOTHER SYMBOLIC VEHICLE—GRAY TO GREEN?

One of the current benefits of being the president of Wheaton College is the privilege of driving a college-owned vehicle. For example, in 2004 Dr. Litfin selected a 2004 Honda Accord to be his presidential vehicle. Typically after three or four years the vehicle is replaced by a newer model, so it was not unexpected that Dr. Litfin would make a vehicle selection in 2007. Since in early 2006 it was announced that he had signed the Evangelical Climate Initiative's *Climate Change: An Evangelical Call to Action*,[21] expressing concern about human-induced causes of global warming and commending the purchase of hybrid vehicles, many people waited to observe the personal and institutional statement Dr. Litfin would be making through this choice, as ESAC had noted in our October 2006 report.

Apparently after considering some hybrid and alternative-fuel vehicles, in June 2007 Dr. Litfin selected, and had the College purchase for his personal use, a 2007 Lexus ES350[22] because "none of those vehicles could satisfy other non-negotiable requirements."[23]

The great difficulty in creation-care decisions lies in the compromises that often must be made with these other requirements. This is the hard work of creation care. In this case, Dr. Litfin decided that other considerations outweighed the environmental impact of his vehicle selection.

Creation-care decisions are not simple or easy. Competing interests and needs must be balanced, and "stewardship" applies to money, time, and other resources as well as to the environment. Wheaton College continues to wrestle with the meaning and application of stewardship principles, but at least we are now wrestling rather than leaving out creation stewardship as a variable.

From gray to green, turning a battleship can be a long, slow process.

---

21. Accessed February 10, 2008. Online: http://www.christiansandclimate.org/

22. The mileage for this vehicle is EPA-listed as 21 miles per gallon (city), 30 (highway); actual tests show a 19.6 to 19.8 miles-per-gallon average. "Use of premium fuel is recommended by Lexus, and is required to get advertised power," according to the manufacturer's Web site at http://www.lexus.com/models/ES/detailed_specifications.html (originally accessed June 14, 2007).

23. As described in an e-mail received by the author on June 14, 2007, from Wheaton College senior vice president, Dr. David Johnston.

APPENDIX A: ESAC THEOLOGICAL BASIS STATEMENT—DRAFT DOCUMENT

The community of believers in Christ at Wheaton College believes and asserts the following theological principles that inform our efforts toward environmental stewardship:

1. Everything that exists was created by God. God made his creation good, and declared it so (Genesis 1:31). It belongs to him (Psalm 24), and he delights in it (Psalm 104). The creation is itself a moral subject of God, with intrinsic value granted to it by God, not dependent on the worth assigned to it by humans. This worth is less than that of humans (Matthew 6:25-26), but nevertheless the creation has intrinsic worth granted by God.

2. Humans have been created "in the image of God" (Genesis 1:27-28). Creation "in the image of God" includes not just *characteristics* or *relationships*, but is also a *position*—the position of chief representative, caretaker and steward of all creation. Humans are to tend the garden, to be regents of creation—"to serve and to keep (protect)" (Genesis 2:15), and have been empowered by God to do so. As Image-Bearers, we are to be focused on God and reflecting his attributes.

3. God has created all things for his own enjoyment, and ours (1 Timothy 6:17). Before humans were sinners, they were stewards (Genesis 2:15). Humans have abused the position of steward, viewing creation as designed not for God's glory but for our autonomous exploitation. Thus we use the entire world selfishly, not to honor Christ its creator, but to consume its benefits for ourselves.

4. Christ has come to reconcile *all* things to himself (Ephesians 1:8-10, Colossians 1:15-20), to redeem all creation from the effects of human sin and the Fall. He calls us, his servants in the world, to engage in the ministry of reconciliation along with him (2 Corinthians 5:18). This reconciliation starts with evangelism and the reconciliation of humans to God, but does not end there. The non-human creation is also included in the reconciliation and redemption of the rest of the created order, such that the effects of human sin are rolled back (Hosea 2, Isaiah 11:1-9).

5. The ushering in of the Kingdom of God will not result in the *destruction* of the created order, but in its *redemption* and reconciliation. All unrighteousness will be purged and the "new heaven and new earth, the home of righteousness," will be *revealed* (2 Peter 3:10–13), along with the true Image-Bearers in all our glory, the reflected glory of God. The creation has been subjected and is groaning, awaiting liberation, not destruction (Romans 8:18–24). There are no eschatological grounds for ignoring creation care.
6. God calls us to creation care, to stewardship—to exert what influence we can to turn the world from consumption on our own behalf to creation stewardship and the celebration of God's glory, in anticipation of the coming revelation of the restored creation and its stewards.

The purpose of our stewardship of God's creation, stewardship done "for Christ and his kingdom," is not to usher in that kingdom ourselves, but to rightly reflect God's intention and will toward the world he has made and to participate in, and demonstrate, his reconciliation and redemption until the final transformation he effects.

APPENDIX B: ESAC STEWARDSHIP COST-BASED DECISION MATRIX—DRAFT DOCUMENT

Environmental stewardship decisions will ask the following priority questions:

1. What need is addressed by the present practice under consideration? Light? Heat? Transportation? Security? Fellowship? Personal growth? Advancement of knowledge? Communication? Comfort? Aesthetics? Etc. What present practices use or effect environmental entities? Physically? Spiritually? Financially?
2. What impact does the current practice have on the environment: Air? Water? Soil? Energy use? Noise? Light? Vibration? Smell? Who and what else is impacted by the current practice: Neighbors? The poor? The economy? How can we measure the volume, rate, extent, etc. of the current practice? What are some good metrics to measure the cost of the present practice? ($ per person, miles per gallon, particles emitted per square foot, etc.) Who bears these costs, and why? How does the present practice affect moral development and formation of virtue?
3. If we seek improvements, how would the success of these be measured?
4. What alternatives to the present practice are available? What are their basic concepts and costs? What are limits on these options—imminence/timeliness? Triage? Instrumental?
5. What impacts would such alternatives have, and how are these measured?
6. What ancillary effects would a change in present practice have? How would the culture of Wheaton College (have to) change to accommodate a different practice? Who are the primary stakeholders in such a change?
7. What would be the best option for solving the problem the present practice addresses? Why is this the best option?

APPENDIX C: ESAC CONSUMPTION-BASED DECISION MATRIX—
DRAFT DOCUMENT

WHAT CAN WE DO?

Initially we should ask:

What is being consumed? (Sort and rank listed items to identify issues of personal or institutional significance that are also actionable.)

Then, for any given item or issue, we should ask:

1. What are the realistic alternatives, or is the consumption avoidable in part or in whole?
2. Is the planned use a part of a normal or natural process, or is it driven by self-centered consumption?
3. Is the item being consumed replaceable with a renewable alternative?
4. Is the impact of the consumption significant? Is it quantifiable?
5. Is the impact of the consumption particularly harmful if it is adopted as common or universal practice?
6. What is our cost of avoiding the consumption or choosing an alternative?
7. Is the cost reasonably affordable (like the concept of reasonable accommodation)?
8. What is the impact of the consumption and/or the alternatives on us and on others?
9. Will we be ignoring an obligation to sacrifice or to demonstrate good stewardship ("to whom much is given, much is required") if we fail to act?
10. What is the right and responsible action regardless of cost and other implications?

EPILOGUE: SO WHAT? NOW WHAT?

Jeffrey K. Greenberg

> "Because in much wisdom there is much grief, and increasing knowledge results in increasing pain" (Eccles 1:18, NASB). "For in many dreams and in many words there is emptiness. Rather, fear God" (Eccles 5:7 NASB).

The bottom line for us is of course to go and do, as we believe our Lord is calling us to act, and not just multiply well-intentioned words. Our duty then is of immense difficulty.

We are to be agents of significant change, not just in theory but in practice. We must seek to make our own lifestyles conform to a more godly pattern before and while we urge others to do the same. From the famous Pogo cartoon strip, the truth is, "*We have met the enemy and he is us.*"[1] We—the writers, speakers, professionals, students, proponents, experts, and zealots of creation care—need to lead by example and pray that the church will follow.

Is the newly reemergent green movement in evangelicalism just a current fad? The church certainly has shown the tendency of modern Western culture in following causes while they are fashionable and then moving on. Our attention span is stunted.

There is reason to be skeptical of the new wave of greening. Apart from evangelicals who are opposed to the movement, there are those of us who can rightfully declare that this is all too familiar. It really didn't result in positive change before, so why get excited now? Perhaps like the older brother in the saga of the Prodigal Son, we who worked hard for this cause over thirty years or so resent those who are now given so much credit for (re)inventing ministry.

---

1. This cartoon by Walt Kelly first appeared in 1970 on an Earth Day poster depicting the Pogo character.

I, for one, am greatly encouraged by the recent stirring among the brethren and sisters. Today's increase of green evangelicals is a substantial growth over those active from the seventies, eighties, and nineties.

The increase has apparently occurred without discernable human plan (no "church-growth" strategies). Previous evangelical advocates were concentrated among academic scientists, a few theologians, and activist communicators. Now there is a strong and growing front among church leaders and leaders in Christian higher education. Certainly the current lot of authors and more prominent voices has built upon a hard-won foundation from their predecessors.

The crucial relationship between solid scientific principles and data, and orthodox theology is accelerating as a wonderful marriage. Sir John Houghton has played an unanticipated role in bringing together expertise of all sorts into a state of agreement, and this catalyst cannot be overemphasized. Houghton's influence upon Rich Cizik of the National Association of Evangelicals has been amplified to include a very impressive list of signatories to the Evangelical Climate Initiative.

Parallel with these leadership proponents, many small organizations in schools and congregations indicate a wider groundswell of support. Ben Lowe's contributions in this volume describe what is happening among college students on evangelical campuses. In this case, unlike in many others, we should be quite pleased that the church is falling in line with a growing trend in our culture.

I certainly do not possess any special gift of prediction. Thankfully, the signs of the times with regard to economics, politics, population dynamics, ecological health, and natural disasters across the globe are not subtle.

Even without a "word of knowledge" or great spiritual sensitivity, I am still capable of foreseeing increasing trouble for life and earth systems with time. But with the worsening that will come from climate alteration, abusive resource exploitation, environmental contamination, and the like, there is also realistic hope for reversal of the degradation.

The current shift toward creation stewardship among God's people is, I believe, another sign. The present momentum represents an incremental step forward for us beyond earlier ministry. My own understanding of the environmental crisis has been refined over the last decade or so, as the evidence for human culpability mounts. The brief essay below is modified from an electronic version posted on the Wheaton College

Center for Applied Christian Ethics Web site (http://www.wheaton.edu/CACE).

If my experience can in any way be taken as a metaphor representing the current movement, then I truly anticipate positive action from the church—action that hopefully includes substantial lifestyle changes.

∽

CLIMATE CHANGE AS A CASE STUDY IN DECIDING

It is time to take sides and get down from our unsteady seat upon the fence.

The tree (of evangelicalism) is being shaken right to its roots. Chuck Colson actually believes that an axe or wedge is being applied to split this tree apart. The recent concern results from the unexpected turn toward a new environmental conscience among biblically and politically conservative Protestants. Colson's "Breakpoint" commentary (Sept. 8, 2006) accuses "liberal" influences of infiltrating the evangelical ranks and using the climate change controversy as a wedge to divide us.

He is right in that this issue finally has the force to divide opinion. He is wrong about the motivation and its source.

Why now a climate change in evangelical understanding? Evangelical environmentalism has been around for a long time but previously failed to make leading pundits pay so much attention. Francis Schaeffer published *Pollution and the Death of Man* back in 1970. Evangelicals for Social Action spawned the Evangelical Environmental Network, and later a coalition of groups formed the Christian Environmental Council (CEC) that met once a year over eight years for fellowship, worship (of the Creator, not of the creation), and mutual support.

Even though the efforts of these meetings were not generally publicized, one initiative did make a big difference. A unified CEC statement on the federal Endangered Species Act (ESA) was delivered to legislators in Congress. The statement—which urged a biblical rationale—supported the ESA and asked that it not be politically weakened. Some politically-conservative members of Congress admitted that the CEC statement from biblically conservative Christians came as a surprise. Washington DC insiders even believe it may have been this support that led to the ESA's renewal. The CEC was not the tool of the political, spiritual, or social Left; most participants typically identified with and voted for Republicans.

Ten years or so later, there is a new momentum among the Jesus-loving, Bible-believing evangelical crowd. Consider "Is God Green?," the recent PBS production in the Bill Moyers series on cultural issues.[2] To distill a key part of the storyline, it shows how a 2002 conference in Oxford, UK, and a follow up in 2004 came to be the inspirations for the Evangelical Climate Initiative.

This is a document signed by a wide array of the perceived leadership among evangelicals. To sign (www.christiansandclimate.org) means an affirmation believing that the great majority of quality science indicates that not only is Earth's overall temperature rising, but it is doing so at a remarkable rate. More importantly, the affirmation is also that (unnecessary) human actions have contributed to the warming and other climate-changing consequences. The initiative calls for serious consideration of our role as responsible stewards of God's world.

At Oxford, Rich Cizik, vice president for government affairs of the National Association of Evangelicals, was compelled to realize the severity of the climate change issue after speaking with Sir John Houghton. Houghton is a highly respected atmospheric physicist, the co-chair of the Intergovernmental Panel on Climate Change, author of many books and articles on the issue, and an outspoken evangelical Christian. Cizik returned home with a zeal to do something of substance about creation-care stewardship.

The drafting of the ECI and its circulation seeking signatories is a story worthy of more space. However, as the initiative gathered support, it also began to attract negative attention from some evangelicals with a history of opposition to proenvironmental action.

There are various themes to the opposition, including an abhorrence of anything that might be identified with "non-Christian" organizations and their agendas. This is a sense of guilt by association that does not seek truth in evaluating issues by their own characteristics.

Note that perhaps the most substantial opposition to setting policy based on climate change dangers is supposedly from science. The argument is that unless scientific data in all its various forms agree and can "prove" greater hazard (costs) in no action than in the measures needed to reduce greenhouse gas emissions, then we should not rock

2. "Is God Green?," produced and directed by Tom Casciato. Broadcast in October 2006 as part of the *Moyers on America* television series on PBS. Accessed February 12, 2008. Online: (http://www.pbs.org/moyers/moyersonamerica/green/index.html).

the boat. Above all other concepts, this argument must be examined and critiqued.

Uncertainty is the excuse. Few will completely deny that human activities can modify the environment. But is it really that big a deal?

Human nature is such that it is easy to convince someone of something when a person is already inclined toward a viewpoint. It is harder to bring the open and unconvinced to a new decision, and all but impossible to change strong convictions with or without hard data as evidence. Scripture's dramatic perspective comes from the words of Jesus: "If they do not listen to Moses and the prophets, they will not be convinced even if one should rise from the dead" (Luke 16:31).

As it turns out, the strongest of the anti-ECI, antienvironmentalism convictions derive from extreme economic and political loyalties. These biases are also worthy of significant examination but distract from the main point. Instead of following today's propensity for vilifying those in opposition, let's attempt a positive support of position.

Our Christian biblical-moral commitments along with scientific confidence constitute the weight of assurance needed to move toward effective action. Justification for this decision begins with physical observation of a multitude of processes operating globally and with the two operators of concern: nature and humanity.

Of course, people are components of the overall grand Earth system. We may be included along with all living actors—earthworms, bacteria, burrowing crustaceans, insects, elephants, molds—and the longer list of mostly abiological processes: glaciers, cyclonic storms, landslides, volcanic eruptions, coastal waves, chemical erosion, and so forth.

Some believe that we need not worry about anthropogenic influence on this world because it is so big and we are relatively so small (and few). Once we can accept that climate change with the current global warming trends is real (again, few deny this), there is still the major contention that change is "natural" and will occur as a consequence of megacycles. Any human-induced alteration would be dwarfed by the regular natural systems.

In testing the hypothesis that humans are not significant agents of change, Professor Hooke and geoscience graduate-students at the University of Maine gathered tremendous amounts of data assessing the extent and cause of physical/chemical change globally each year.[3] After significant review by other earth scientists, the very comprehensive research was acknowledged to indicate that people are as effective (for better or worse) in modifying the land, sea, and air as all the other factors combined.

We are indeed very much a special creation, with the ability to unilaterally convert the desert to garden and the garden to desert.

Given our status as unique actors, consider some of the cases in which humans have actually caused climatic alterations on regional scales. There is no doubt that within a single human generation, vast tracts of land in Tanzania south of Lake Victoria have been transformed from lush forest to degraded, arid wasteland. World Vision filmed a tribal elder living in the region since birth. In his memory, there has been deforestation and the loss of through-flowing streams, loss of virtually all mammals and most birds, loss of fertile soil, and loss of the seasonal rainfall events that maintained the environment.

The regional degradation was not a coincidence of natural change over seventy years or so. It was very obviously initiated by poor land-use practices, and deeply injured people as well as other life precious to its Creator.

This East African saga is reminiscent of *The Man Who Planted Trees*,[4] a brilliant story by Jean Giono published in 1985. The same scenario of human-modifying loss can be documented for many, many places on Earth. Open any larger text on environmental science or environmental geology and you can see myriad testimonies, often with photos of degradation.

Following the above realizations, we then may take a fairly safe leap of faith scientifically to relate the additive effect of thousands of macro-examples on the megasystem of Earth climate. The real burden of proof should not be on those warning of our culpability in harming God's good Earth. It should be on the antienvironmental thinkers to argue their position: to show that the ways we have behaved and continue to behave have *not* been a heavy blow to the health of the planet and its creatures.

If by any reasonable chance we are responsible for unwisely or selfishly manipulating the environment, then it is our biblical mandate as the

---

3. See R. L. Hooke, On the efficacy of humans as geomorphic agents, *GSA Today* 4 (1994) 217, 224–25; R. L. Hooke, On the history of humans as geomorphic agents, *Geology* 28 (2000) 843–46.

4. Jean Giono, *The Man Who Planted Trees* (Chelsea, VT: Chelsea Green, 1985).

Master's caretakers to fix the problems as well as we are able. Can we not at least agree upon that? This version of the cautionary principle counters selfish interests and may mean that our treasured affluent lifestyles need alteration.

To further the call for a decision, we might need to be reminded that unarguable "proof" is extremely rare in any reality. People actually live as probability thinkers. This is to say what most scientists well understand: confidence comes in proportions. If we knew that air travel was safe 51 percent of the time and fatal 49 percent of the time, then how many would accept the risk?

Of course this is true for many circumstances, but not all. A crucial election can be won with 51 percent of the vote (or perhaps less), and yet we may be subject then to someone with actual power over life and death. Even though the vast majority of cases where abortions are elected without real threat to maternal life in this country, only 2 percent or so of the harder cases are emphasized to justify keeping existing law.[5]

The raw data and percentages pointing one way or the other don't tell all of the story. Why do some opponents of proenvironmental legislation, regulation, preservation, and even conservation ask for proof? I am convinced without so-called proof.

When the Evangelical Environmental Network first circulated its petition "An Evangelical Declaration on the Care of Creation" in 1994, the wording was such that some of us, especially in science, could not sign it. After wise revision and now with even stronger supporting evidence, signing on seems like an important spiritual duty.

The most controversial section in the 1994 document concerns global climate change. Twelve years later, the issue has come due for advocacy among God's people. The ECI offers us a chance to unite and show the world that we do truly care about more than just heaven and proscribing what is sinful in others. Positive measures to individually and corporately repent of our hurtful attitudes and practices are available from various sources, including the Pew Center on Global Climate Change (www.pewclimate.org).

∽

---

5. See, for example, Curt Young, *The Least of These* (Chicago: Moody, 1983); or Dr. J. C. Willke and Mrs. J. C. Willke, *Abortion: Questions and Answers* (Cincinnati: Hayes, 1988).

Acceptance of the reality of human-induced climate alteration may be the biggest hurdle in accomplishing an enduring role as evangelical stewards. And there is an exhilarating sense that the hurdle is essentially behind us. We look forward to the immense potential of mobilized Christians as agents of transformation.

To those who are concerned about joining our intentions with an unbelievers' agenda, please judge our motives by God's word and not by political rhetoric. In fact, consider the wonderful effect on non-Christians when they realize that we actually do love creation or "nature" as much or more than they do.

Consider also the potential for creation-care ministries across the Earth as the core of powerful missionary outreach. The whole gospel comes as we promote sanitation, clean water, fertile soil and other sustainable resources for the poor. The physical reality is that if the environment is "sick," so shall the people be. Kristen Page describes how degraded ecosystems can release pathogenic organisms and spread horrible new plagues.[6]

Students of perceptive mind and sensitive conscience never allow me to conclude a lecture on environmental "gloom and doom" without relief. They always expect to find out what can be done to reverse harm to creation. Romans 8:19–22 speaks to us as the Lord's own voice in our present and future agency of reconciliation. In these verses, we are shown to be what a suffering ("groaning") world is waiting for.

This world is not just the human essence of creation, but it includes everything as God made it. My optimism is that perhaps we are now on the edge of a new Holy-Spirit awakening—a revival as such. This time, the fruits of revival will include creation care.

Specific elements of a fruitful ministry shall involve, as mentioned above, modifying our own lifestyles. Individuals and groups desiring to move forward may join existing organizations of Christians or others already making a difference in energy utilization or purchasing practices. To cite two examples, Christian students and church congregants can organize actions either to offer reusable grocery bags or to promote use of most tap-water supplies, over the public hysteria of bottled water. There is no scarcity of ideas and opportunities available for positive ac-

---

6. See, for example, L. Kristen Page, "Ecology and Transmission Dynamics of *Baylisascaris procyonis*" (PhD dissertation, Purdue University, 1998). Accessed February 12, 2008. Online: http://docs.lib.purdue.edu/dissertations/AAI9914534/

tion—just do an Internet search! Potential is enormous. I pray that our leaders in the church, both the popular parachurch personalities and our own congregational shepherds, will gain inspiration and courage to lead us into the work ahead.

For those feeling the desire to help but also feeling helpless: cheer up! For most of us, this middle-class society has a certain rigid hold, restricting the way we live and how much we can accomplish. This condition is more self-committed than imposed. Change is possible.

Two age groups of people in the U.S. are a lot freer than we might believe. Young people of roughly college age should be able to plan at least the basic framework of their career direction. They can decide and strive to be placed in strategic areas of ministry, broadly construed. They may choose between goals of greater financial gain and greater usefulness in the kingdom.

Today ministry needs to occur in all the myriad ways that humans relate to each other, to other forms of life, and to the inanimate environment. I wish that Christian students would research the avenues in which their chosen field of study could contribute as directly to "kingdom" work as possible. My own area (earth science) has become incredibly important in global application.

The other age group with unique potential to make a difference is the empty nesters, those nearing retirement. Many of us have more time and resources available for ministry now than at any other phase of life. We can go and do. Many have extremely well-honed skills that are useful here and abroad. The ideal of having a huge, beautiful home and lots of leisure time for golf, cruises, and the like should not ensnare us. This ought to bring a new season of expectation—not the beginning of the end!

For the younger folk and the older folk, Ben Lowe and Sir John Houghton can be role models. These are missionaries to our evangelical culture, and they are devoted to bringing a strong biblical message of repentance. Other forms of dynamic mission work have multiplied in our time, especially because of human relationships with the environment. In contrast to the past traditional paradigm of missionary service (i.e., the Bible college or seminary-trained evangelist and church planter), we now are drawn to contribute what the blessings of an affluent West have invested in us.

We have immense reserves of financial wealth, quite in spite of how our consumer mentalities might impress us otherwise. More godly lifestyles will surely free up funds to support the Lord's global agenda. We are also very richly endowed with education. A college degree has become a standard for us as the majority of the world continues to struggle at getting those children who survive the first five years of life into primary school. Our learning is another valuable commodity to share with the needy.

Consider how we might follow the Timothy 2:2 pattern: teaching others what we know so that they in turn can become trainers and can multiply the benefits where most needed. This newer form of holistic missions need not be invented. It already exists in notable examples.

Lifewater International is a volunteer organization of Christian geologists and engineers (www.lifewater.org) called to transform areas without clean, adequate supplies of potable water. They bring a rugged and easily-maintained drill rig to villages and spend enough time to train local people to complete successful wells. Once trained to oversee the entire water production enterprise, the locals train other responsible individuals. The drilling equipment is then given to the new indigenous trainers.

In every venture, a strong, indigenous church base is established to help ensure project sustainability. The provision of physical water is always the focus of an evangelistic ceremony for the surrounding region. The Lifewater people come, do their work with establishment of continuity, and then move on. This is perhaps a version of apostolic ministry along the pattern that Paul exercised in his travels. Funds are needed for the equipment and for the "missionary" travel and subsistence. Training trainers is the bottom line.

There should be no reason to exclude all sorts of other practical-knowledge transfers from the West to the majority world. Of course, there are many organizations established to carry out such a transfer, but there is a difference. Megafunding bodies, including USAID, the World Bank, and foundations like the Bill and Melinda Gates Foundation are highly political and operate at upper levels of society. Bang-per-buck financial effectiveness of these organizations is highly suspect. There are also secular vehicles like the Peace Corps to bring more grassroots help to the needy around the globe.

All these entities are deficient in their lack of ultimate spiritual foundation. I have to believe that God's family can do it better, and we are charged to offer compassionate service in Christ's name. In the 1980s,

Tom Sine used the title *The Mustard Seed Conspiracy* to urge a groundswell of the Christian multitudes to go and do. Sine's book was an inspiration for many of us.[7] His message applies more now than when it was popular.

---

7. Tom Sine, *The Mustard Seed Conspiracy: You Can Make a Difference in Tomorrow's Troubled World* (Waco TX: Word, 1981).

CONTRIBUTORS

Douglas Allen is a professor at Dordt College, where he teaches classes in physics, astronomy, and environmental studies. He graduated with a BS in physics from Wheaton College and a PhD in atmospheric physics from Iowa State University. Prior to teaching, Allen spent a combined eight years in research at NASA Goddard Space Flight Center, at the University of Chicago, and at the Naval Research Lab. His research interests involve studying large-scale atmospheric dynamics and transport using global numerical models and satellite observations of the Earth's atmosphere.

Jeffrey K. Greenberg has been teaching geology at Wheaton College for over twenty-one years. He also was the founder of Wheaton's environmental science program. He has a great passion for utilizing the academic disciplines as vehicles for global transformation and believes that faculty should prepare young people to be those agents of Christ's transforming love. In Jeff's specific case, water, soil and mineral resources, natural-hazard reduction, and appropriate land-use practices have become main themes of ministry. Eastern Africa and South Africa have become the foci of his ministry projects.

P. J. Hill is George F. Bennett Professor of Economics at Wheaton College, and a Senior Fellow at PERC (the Property and Environment Research Center) in Bozeman, Montana. He has coauthored many books, including *Growth and Welfare in the American Past* and *The Birth of a Transfer Society*. He has also authored numerous articles on the theory of property rights and institutional change, and has edited six books on environmental economics. His undergraduate degree is from Montana State University and his PhD from the University of Chicago. P. J. grew up in eastern Montana on a cattle ranch that he operated with his family until 1992, when he sold the ranch and bought a smaller ranch in western Montana that he continues to operate.

Sir John T. Houghton's early scientific career was at Oxford University, where he led a research group developing instrumentation for observations of the Earth's atmosphere from NASA's Nimbus satellites; he was professor of atmospheric physics (1976–1983). He became Director General (later Chief Executive) of the UK Meteorological Office in 1983, where he took a particular interest in research into human-induced climate change; and in 1988, on the formation of the Intergovernmental Panel on Climate Change, he was appointed chairman of its scientific assessment—a position he held until 2002. After retiring from the Met Office in 1991, he became chairman of the Royal Commission on Environmental Pollution (1992–1998); chairman of the John Ray Initiative, a charity formed to connect science, environment, and Christianity in the promotion of environmental sustainability (1997–); and a trustee of the Shell Foundation (2000–). He continues to lecture widely on climate change, on the underlying science, and on the challenge it presents to all human communities. His many awards include the Japan Prize (2006), the International Meteorological Organisation Prize (1998), gold medals from the Royal Astronomical Society and the Royal Meteorological Society, and honorary degrees of Doctor of Science from a number of universities, including Oxford (2006). His books include *The Physics of Atmospheres, Global Warming: the Complete Briefing, Does God Play Dice?* and *The Search for God: Can Science Help?* He now lives in Aberdyfi, Wales, where he enjoys sailing and mountain walking.

A. Duane Litfin holds a PhD from Purdue University and a DPhil from Oxford University. He is serving in his fifteenth year as the president of Wheaton College. Author of numerous articles and books (most recently, *Conceiving the Christian College*), Litfin was one of the original signatories to the Evangelical Climate Initiative (ECI) statement, "Climate Change: An Evangelical Call to Action."

Born and raised as a missionary kid in South East Asia, **Ben Lowe** graduated from Wheaton College in 2007 with a BS in environmental studies.

While at Wheaton he served as the president of the A Rocha student chapter for two years and organized the first national student creation-care summit with Sir John Houghton (The Wheaton Summit). He now works as the outreach director for Christians in Conservation/A Rocha USA. A Rocha is an international Christian conservation organization working in over sixteen countries, and Ben's main focus is to develop and support student creation-care initiatives on campuses and in churches throughout the United States. He speaks to diverse audiences on the biblical importance and contemporary urgency of creation care and is the author of a book on the next generation of Christian environmental stewardship, to be published by InterVarsity Press in 2008.

After an enjoyable decade as a youth minister, in 1998 **Vincent E. Morris** came to work at Wheaton College, where he became the director of risk management. His days are filled with general troubleshooting and managing a wide variety of risks similar to those of a small city. Along with a handful of risk-management certifications, Vince holds an MBA in finance and strategy from the University of Chicago and an MA in theology from the Wheaton College Graduate School, where he wrote a thesis exploring the involvement of evangelicals in environmental movements—or the lack thereof. In 2005 he was appointed by Wheaton College president Duane Litfin to form and chair the Environmental Stewardship Advisory Committee at Wheaton College, a group charged with the tasks of 1) determining how Wheaton College is doing on creation care, 2) determining what "best practices" for creation care at Christian institutions might be, and 3) recommending changes to move the college from where we are to where we should be.

L. Kristen Page received her MS degree from Auburn and her PhD from Purdue University. She teaches biology at Wheaton College, where she encourages her students to consider their Christian response to environmental challenges. Her research interests focus on disease ecology, specifically on how disease transmission responds to changing landscapes.

Lindy Scott holds a PhD from Northwestern University and two masters degrees from Trinity Evangelical Divinity School. He is currently professor of Spanish and Latin American studies at Whitworth University in Spokane, Washington. He previously taught at Wheaton College for twelve years, where he also directed the Center for Applied Christian Ethics. Lindy is the editor of the *Journal of Latin American Theology: Christian Reflections from the Latino South* and has authored numerous books, including *Terrorism and the War in Iraq: A Christian Word from Latin America.*

Noah J. Toly is director of urban studies and assistant professor of politics and international relations at Wheaton College. He teaches urban and environmental politics, and his research interests lie at the intersection of the two. He is especially concerned with environmental justice in the relationship between cities and the global environment, including cities and climate politics. Before joining the faculty at Wheaton, Noah was a policy fellow at the University of Delaware's Center for Energy and Environmental Policy. A graduate of Wheaton College, Noah holds an MA and a PhD in Urban Affairs and Public Policy from the University of Delaware.

INDEX

adaptation, role of, in addressing climate change, 53
Agenda 21, 54
Alliance of Small Island States (AOSIS), 51
A Rocha International, 88–89
A Rocha Wheaton, 83, 87, 88, 108, 115
Asia Pacific Partnership on Clean Development and Climate (APPCDC), 57
atmosphere-ocean system, internal variation on, 14

Bacote, Vince, 81
bacterial pathogens, 30–31
Ball, Jim, 89
Berry, Wendell, 91–92
Bhagwati, Jagdish, 40
Big Bang, 68–69
biodiversity loss, 50
Boyle, Richard, 74
Brief History of Time, A (Hawking), 72
Brown, Ken, 95

Calvin, John, 102–3
cap-and-trade policy, 45n27
carbon dioxide, 16–17, 19
Center for Applied Christian Ethics (Wheaton College), 115
cholera, 30–31

Christian colleges, role of, in environmental awareness, 92–93
Christian Environmental Council, 126
Christianity, priorities within, 104–5
Christians, called to care for creation, 80–81
Cities for Climate Protection (International Council on Local Environmental Initiatives), 57–58
Cizik, Rich, 125, 127
Clark, Jim, 80
Cleary, Leo, 95–96, 108
climate
  direct impact of, on human health, 26–28
  direct and indirect observations of, 9
  related to seasonal emergence of disease, 28–29
  vs. weather, 7
climate change. *See also* global warming
  adverse effects of, 50–53
  anthropogenic nature of, 48
  as case study in deciding, 126–34
  confusing surrounding debate about, 7–8
  data on, 72
  deaths resulting from, 51–52

139

climate change (*continued*)
  defining, 7
  disproportionate effect of, on Global South, 25
  dispute over cause of, 48
  evidence of, 48
  global causes of, 47–49
  global consequences of, 50–53
  global solutions for, 53–58
  indirect impacts of, on human health, 31–32
  opposition to policy about, sources of, 127–28
  political-economy issues of dealing with, 43
  in preindustrial era, 47–48
  proposals for, ranked among methods for advancing global welfare, 42
  response to, 33
  scientists' role in debate about, 9–10
  as security issue, 52
"Climate Change: An Evangelical Call to Action," 110, 118. *See also* Evangelical Climate Initiative (ECI)
climate models, 18–21
Climate Protection Agreement (United States Conference of Mayors), 57
climate system
  complexity of, 8
  models of, 10
  threat of changes to, 6
climate variables, defining, 7
Clouser, Roy, 8
coal, as energy source, 82
Collins, Francis, 71
Colson, Chuck, 126
community, building and living in, 90–92
conflict, related to climate change and human suffering, 52

Conradie, Ernst, 105
consciousness, 73
Convention on Biological Diversity (CBD), 54
Cook, David, 80
Copenhagen Consensus, 40–42
Corts, Paul, 89
Cowper, William, 75–76
creation
  degradations of, 99–100
  role of humans in, 105–6
  suffering, 34
creation care, 80–81
  Christian perspective on, 97–99
  ministries for, 131–34
  shift toward, 125–26

Dawkins, Richard, 70, 73
Dawson, Tony, 111
debt-for-nature swaps, 45
deforestation, 45
deist God, 70, 72
DeWitte, Calvin, 99–100
disease, related to climate, 28–29
Doty, Greg, 111
drought, health effects of, 27–28
Dunn, Britney, 88

Earth, variation in orbit of, 13
Earth Summit, 54
economics, importance of, to global environmental framework, 36
ecosystem
  function of, human health associated with, 24
  human alteration of, 25–26
Einstein, Albert, 70
emissions abatement, 55–56
emissions trading, 55–56
Emmerich, Susan, 89
Endangered Species Act, 126
enhanced greenhouse effect, 6
entropy, 69

environmental degradation, burden of proof regarding, 129–30
environmental injustice, 58
eschatology, as reason for avoiding creation care, 101–2
Evangelical Climate Initiative (ECI), 3–4, 93, 110, 118, 127, 130. *See also* "Climate Change: An Evangelical Call to Action"
Evangelical Environmental Network, 126, 130
evangelicals, shying away from environmental movements, 99
Evangelicals for Social Action, 126

Fagan, Reed, 88
fishing, worldwide, 43–44, 104n12
flooding, health effects of, 27
Fogel, Robert, 40
Fourth Assessment Report (FAR) (IPCC), 10, 11
Frey, Bruno, 40
future, difficulty of predicting, 38–39

Giono, Jean, 129
global climate governance, interpreting, 58–59
global commons, 43–44
global warming. *See also* climate change
  altering ecosystem processes, 24
  biblical themes related to, 36
  capacity for adaptation to, unevenly distributed, 53
  causes of, 13–18, 49
  consequences of, 21–22
  costs and benefits of dealing with, 38–40
  defining, 7
  determining Christian response to, 36
  evidence for, 10–12
  health risks related to, 29
  possible benefits of, 29

global warming (*continued*)
  potential anthropogenic causes of, in twentieth century, 15–18
  potential natural causes of, in twentieth century, 13–15
  subsidies increasing the risk of harm from, 45
  testing of, through climate models, 18–21
  time involved in estimating effects of, 38
global welfare, methods of advancing, 40–42
God
  characteristics of, 72–73
  deist, 70, 72
  personal, 72–73, 74
  wisdom of, in works of creation, 75
  works and Word of, 74–75
God Delusion, The (Dawkins), 73
Goklany, Indur, 42
Gordon College, 95, 108–9
Great Commission, 80
Greenberg, Jeff, 80, 82
greenhouse effect, 6, 15–18
greenhouse gases, 6, 16–20, 21, 49
greening
  Christian perspective on, 97–99
  skepticism surrounding, 124

hantavirus pulmonary syndrome (HPS), 28–29
Harris, Miranda, 108n17
Harris, Peter, 108n17
Hart, Abby, 88
Hawking, Stephen, 72–73
health, climate's direct impact on, 26–28
heat-wave analysis, 52–53
Hill, P. J., 80, 111
Houghton, John, 86–87, 89–90, 115, 125, 127, 132

Index

human health
  associated with ecosystem function, 24
  current state of, 24–25
  indirect impacts of climate on, 31–32
humans
  made in God's image, 69–70
  role of, in creation, 105–6
human suffering, from climate change, 51–52
Huxley, Thomas, 72

Individual Transferable Quotas (ITQs), 43–44
industrializing nations, greenhouse gases from, 49–50
industrial revolution, ongoing effects of, 49
infectious diseases, trends in, linked to ecological change, 25–26
intelligent design, 70–71
Intergovernmental Panel on Climate Change (IPCC), 10, 32–33, 49, 71–72
International Solar Cities Initiative, 57, 58
International Whaling Commission, 44n22

Johnson, Jim, 111
Johnston, David, 118
Jutsum, Lisa, 88

Koeningsberg, Bruce, 111
Kyoto Protocol, 37–38, 54–59

Lake Victoria (Tanzania), 129
Language of God, The (Collins), 71
Lifewater International, 133
Lin, Justin Yifu, 40
Litfin, Duane, 87, 89, 107, 108–9, 113, 119
Little Ice Age, 12, 14

Lomborg, Bjørn, 40, 42
Lowe, Ben, 108, 111, 115, 118, 125, 132
Luedtke, Jennifer, 88

malaria, 29–30
malnutrition, 28
Man Who Planted Trees, The (Giono), 129
Mead, Steve, 111
Medieval Warm Period, 12
methane, 16–17
Milankovitch cycles, 13
Montreal Protocol, 54
Moo, Douglas, 101
Morris, Ellen, 88
Morris, Vince, 88, 111
mountaintopping, 82
Myers, Norman, 50

Nash, James, 100
natural theology, 73
nature worship, fear of, 102–3
Newton, Isaac, 74
Newton, John, 75
Nieves, Alvaro, 80
nitrous oxide, 16–17
Nordhaus, William, 39–40
Norquist, Bruce, 111
nuclear power, 44–45

Olney Hymns, 75
open-access resource, 43

paganism, fear of, 102–3
Page, Kristen, 80, 131
panentheism, fear of, 102–3
pantheism, 102–3n9
Payne, Brendan, 88
Penrose, Roger, 69
plants, productivity of, 31
plate tectonics, 13
policy argument, vs. scientific argument, 8

Pollution and the Death of Man
(Schaeffer), 126
poor populations
disproportionate effects of climate
change on, 52–53
effect on, of restricting carbon
emissions, 40, 44
most significant environmental
problems for, 37
population displacement, 32

radiative forcing, 18–20
Ray, John, 74
Regional Greenhouse Gas Initiative,
57
religious beliefs, filtering scientific
data, 8
Richmond, Lisa, 111
Riihimaki, Lisa, 88
Rio Declaration on Environment and
Development, 54
Rorem, Nadine, 80
Rossi, Vincent, 102

Samuelson, Robert, 4
Schaeffer, Francis, 126
Schelling, Thomas, 40
science-religion connection, 71, 74
scientists
methods of, for dissemination
information, 10
public's expectations of, 9
role of, in debate about climate
change, 9–10
sea-level rise, 20–21, 32, 50–51
self-awareness, 73
*Sex, Economy, Freedom, and
Community* (Berry), 91–92
Sharman, Glenn, 88
Singapore, 78
Sleeth, Matthew, 89
Smith, Vernon, 40
social values, loss of, 50
solar variability, 14–15

species extinction, 50
Stern Report, 4. *See also* Stern
Review
Stern Review, estimating cost of
global warming, 38–40
Stokey, Nancy, 40
sulfate aerosols, 17, 20
sulfur dioxide, 17
sunspots, 14
sustainability, 97

temperature, role of, in
seasonal plant cycles and
photosynthesis, 31
Temple, William, 73
Third Assessment Report (TAR)
(IPCC), 10
trade-offs, related to global
environmental framework,
37–38
tragedy of the commons, 43
tree-hugging, understandings of,
77, 84
truth, objective, 75

United Nations Conference
on Environment and
Development (UNCED), 54
United Nations Framework
Convention on Climate
Change (UNFCCC), 54
United Nations Security Council, 52
universe
beginning of, 68
comprehensibility of, 69–70
dimensions of, 68
precision in, 68–69

van Dyke, Fred, 80, 89, 108, 110–11
vectorborne diseases, seasonal
patterns of, 29
Venus, greenhouse effect on, 67
volcanoes, 14

weather, vs. climate, 7
Western Governors Association, 57
whaling, 44n22
Wheaton College, 4, 79–81, 83
   creation-care responsibilities of, 107
   Environmental Stewardship Advisory Committee, 109–23
   greening of, 96–98
   growing environmental awareness at, 87–90, 92, 93–94
   priorities of, 107–10
   public health crisis and environmental disaster at, 85–86
   recommendations for changes at, 117–18
   Statement of Faith, 98–99, 106
Wheaton Summit, 86–90, 92, 93–94, 115–16
White, Lynn, 104
Wilcoxson, Aaron, 88
women's health, affected by population displacement, 32
worldviews, affecting perception of data, 8
Wren, Christopher, 74

www.ingramcontent.com/pod-product-compliance
Lightning Source LLC
Chambersburg PA
CBHW072143160426
43197CB00012B/2222